A GIFT FOR:

FROM:

REFLECTIONS OF HOPE

A 90-Day Devotional Journey

Recognize and Recover from the
Cycle of Toxic Broken Relationships

By
Kimberly A. Sanford

Copyright © 2021 by Breakthrough Publications and © 2021 Kimberly A. Sanford

ALL RIGHTS RESERVED. This book contains material protected under International and Federal Laws and Treaties. Any unauthorized reprint or use of this material is prohibited. No portion of this book may be used, reproduced, stored in a retrieval system, or transmitted in any form or by any means — electronic, mechanical, photocopy, recording, scanning, or other — without express written permission from the author or publisher, except for a brief quotation in critical reviews or articles. It is illegal to copy this book, post it to a website, or distribute it by any other means without permission from the author and publisher.

Published by

Breakthrough Publications
Dallas, Texas

Copyright Use and Public Information

Unless otherwise noted, images have been used according to public information laws.

ISBN: **978-0-578-86102-9**   Paperback

Limits of Liability and Disclaimer of Warranty

The author and publisher shall not be liable for the reader's misuse of this material. This book is for strictly informational and educational purposes.

Scripture quotations taken from the New American Standard Bible® (NASB), Copyright © 1960, 1962, 1963, 1968, 1971, 1972, 1973, 1975, 1977, 1995 by The Lockman Foundation Used by permission. www.Lockman.org. The Holy Bible, English Standard Version® (ESV®) Copyright © 2001 by Crossway, a publishing ministry of Good News Publishers. All rights reserved. Scriptures marked NLT are taken from the HOLY BIBLE, NEW LIVING TRANSLATION (NLT): Scriptures taken from the HOLY BIBLE, NEW LIVING TRANSLATION, Copyright© 1996, 2004, 2007 by Tyndale House Foundation. Used by permission of Tyndale House Publishers, Inc., Carol Stream, Illinois 60188. All rights reserved. Used by permission. Scriptures marked NIV are taken from the NEW INTERNATIONAL VERSION (NIV): Scripture taken from THE HOLY BIBLE, NEW INTERNATIONAL VERSION ®. Copyright© 1973, 1978, 1984, 2011 by Biblica, Inc.™. Used by permission of Zondervan. Scriptures marked TM are taken from the THE MESSAGE: THE BIBLE IN CONTEMPORARY ENGLISH (TM): Scripture taken from THE MESSAGE: THE BIBLE IN CONTEMPORARY ENGLISH, copyright©1993, 1994, 1995, 1996, 2000, 2001, 2002. Used by permission of NavPress Publishing Group. Scriptures marked AMP are taken from the AMPLIFIED BIBLE (AMP): Scripture taken from the AMPLIFIED® BIBLE, Copyright © 1954, 1958, 1962, 1964, 1965, 1987 by the Lockman Foundation Used by Permission. Scriptures marked HCSB are taken from the HOLMAN CHRISTIAN STANDARD BIBLE (HCSB): Scripture taken from the HOLMAN CHRISTIAN STANDARD BIBLE, copyright© 1999, 2000, 2002, 2003 by Holman Bible Publishers, Nashville Tennessee. All rights reserved. Scriptures marked CEV are taken from the CONTEMPORARY ENGLISH VERSION (CEV): Scripture taken from the CONTEMPORARY ENGLISH VERSION copyright© 1995 by the American Bible Society. Used by permission. Scriptures marked KJV are taken from the KING JAMES VERSION (KJV): KING JAMES VERSION, public domain.

Disclaimer

The views expressed are those of the author and do not reflect the official policy or position of the publisher. This publication is designed to provide accurate and authoritative information regarding the subject matter covered. It is sold with the understanding that both the author and the publisher are not engaged in rendering legal, accounting, clinical or other professional advice. If legal advice or other expert assistance is required, the services of a competent professional should be sought. The opinions expressed by the author in this book are not endorsed by Breakthrough Publishing and are the sole responsibility of the author rendering the opinion.

I dedicate this book to my Lord and Savior without Whom my life would be completely different, and I couldn't have written it.

I also dedicate this book to my two beautiful daughters – Kayla and Kelsey and to my wonderful grandchildren Keith (my munchkin), Emma (my love bug), Cody (my Li'l buddy), and Hunter (my baby love).

Last but certainly not least, I dedicate this book to my Dad – David Sanford, and to my Mom – Sharon Sanford, who passed away prior to the publishing of this book. Mom, I miss you very much.

TABLE OF CONTENTS

Day 1	Soul Ties	1
Day 2	Standing at a Crossroad	4
Day 3	Suffering	7
Day 4	Spirit, Soul, and Body	10
Day 5	Spirit Commanded	13
Day 6	Your Soul	16
Day 7	Your Body	18
Day 8	Appointments	20
Day 9	Trust the Process	22
Day 10	Discipline	24
Day 11	Accountability	26
Day 12	When Hope Hurts	28
Day 13	Discernment	31
Day 14	Grieving	33
Day 15	Pursued	35
Day 16	Attraction	37
Day 17	Growth	39
Day 18	Pruning	41
Day 19	Doubt	43
Day 20	Gains and Losses	45

Day 21	Trauma Bond	48
Day 22	Trust	51
Day 23	Lessons	54
Day 24	Get Up	56
Day 25	Feeling Stuck	58
Day 26	Self-Worth	60
Day 27	Progress not Perfection	63
Day 28	Your Assignment	66
Day 29	Loneliness	68
Day 30	The Journey	71
Day 31	Retrain Your Brain	74
Day 32	Finding Joy	76
Day 33	Self-Awareness	78
Day 34	Transformation	80
Day 35	Plant Yourself	82
Day 36	Be an Influence	84
Day 37	The Wrath	86
Day 38	Right Place, Right Time	88
Day 39	Stand Firm	90
Day 40	Love Yourself	92
Day 41	Seeking	95
Day 42	Renovations Underway	97

Day 43	Healing Through Tears	101
Day 44	Sword of the Spirit	103
Day 45	Encouragement	105
Day 46	Shifting your Perspective	108
Day 47	Childhood Breakthroughs	110
Day 48	Validation and Approval-Seeking	113
Day 49	Fixing	115
Day 50	Patience	117
Day 51	Disappointment	119
Day 52	Childhood Losses	121
Day 53	Anxiety	124
Day 54	Personal Boundaries	126
Day 55	Codependency	129
Day 56	Emotional Honesty	132
Day 57	Confidence	134
Day 58	Power of Words	136
Day 59	Trusting Again	139
Day 60	Recognizing Change	141
Day 61	Hidden Wounds	144
Day 62	Fighting Battles	147
Day 63	Focus on the Future	149
Day 64	Love	151

Day 65	Do Unto Others	154
Day 66	Putting in Time	156
Day 67	Energy Leak	159
Day 68	Invalidation	161
Day 69	The Enemy	163
Day 70	Evaluating the Self	166
Day 71	Impostor Syndrome	168
Day 72	Enabling Pain	171
Day 73	Love Addiction	174
Day 74	Love Avoidant	177
Day 75	Enmeshment	179
Day 76	Who I Am	181
Day 77	Above and Beyond	184
Day 78	The Storm	187
Day 79	Sitting with God	189
Day 80	God's Favor	191
Day 81	Perfectionism	193
Day 82	Narcissism	196
Day 83	"Crazy"-Making	199
Day 84	Grace and Gratitude	202
Day 85	Sex	205
Day 86	Abandonment	208

Day 87	Sincerity	210
Day 88	Emotional Sobriety	212
Day 89	Authenticity	214
Day 90	Potential	217

Recommended Resources	219
Kimberly A. Sanford	221
Please Rate My Book	223

Day 1

SOUL TIES

*I*t's painful, it seems like it will never end, and your mind tells you that you can't make it without *that* relationship. You excessively think about, long for, and have an intense desire to connect; yet, you are confused and *miserable* in the relationship. You try leaving…but keep going back.

Soul ties are *extremely* powerful.

The Bible speaks of soul ties when it refers to the knitting together of souls and two becoming one flesh. It's a bond that connects you to someone. So, soul ties are meant for our good to unite us in ways such as marriage as seen in Ephesians 5:31 where it tells us "two will become one flesh," or in friendship as found in 1 Samuel 18:1 where "the soul of Jonathan was knit with the soul of David, and Jonathan loved him as his own soul."

But ungodly soul ties are formed when sin enters in and allows the enemy to use what is meant for good against us. This can be through an affair, pre-marital sex, unhealthy spoken vows, or anything we allow to take greater authority over our lives than God. When soul ties are formed, we become emotionally attached. So, an ungodly soul tie can seem impossible to escape from.

I know first-hand what it's like to break free from an ungodly soul tie. Sin entered my relationship as I allowed other things to take greater authority over my life than God. As things steadily declined in the relationship, I reached a point where I began to question if I even liked the person I was with. Yet I would defend him and our relationship to others. I would decide to leave but the intensity to connect again would drive me back. It was confusing *even* to me.

I knew that confusion, disorder, and a lack of peace in my relationship meant that God was not the center of it. I asked God for clarity and a vision for my future. This began a personal and spiritual growth and recovery journey, and I worked toward becoming the best version of myself while setting and crushing goals.

Are you ready to stop looking back except to see how far you have come? Are you ready to break the stronghold from ungodly soul ties? This journey begins when you repent and allow God to have authority over your life. It is through the power of prayer and repentance that we can be empowered to overcome.

For God is not a God of disorder but of peace, as in all the meetings of God's holy people. 1 Corinthians 14:33 (NLT)

Day 2

STANDING AT A CROSSROAD

When you come to a crossroad, will you choose the road less traveled? The road less traveled is the unfamiliar one, it's often very uncomfortable and requires that you learn a new way. However, along with it comes a change of scenery that brings awareness to a beautiful new place that awaits once you let go of the old way. It's about committing to a new journey.

I found myself standing at the same crossroad many times as I *repeatedly* chose the **wrong way**. I questioned if I would ever stop going back down that same familiar road. My feelings and emotions caused me to question whether things were really *that* bad, and I continued to justify this **wrong way**. These same emotions caused me to focus only on the "good," and in my weakness, I continued to choose the same familiar path expecting it to lead somewhere new.

I mistakenly continued to think each time might be different, possibly repairs had been made to that road or I could work around the damage that was still there. I wish I could say that this was true, but I can't count the number of times I stumbled down that same familiar road expecting it to lead somewhere different…only to end in the same *wrong* place.

When I committed to taking the road less traveled, I found myself asking why it was so difficult. If this was the right way, I wondered why it felt so wrong and how long it would be until I reached a new place.

I thought if there was a deadline I could strive for, a point in time where I knew it would end, I could get there easier. I thought the feelings I had would *never* change, but every time I ignored God's direction and traveled down the road I wanted, I fell into the same potholes, suffered more damage, and found it even *more* difficult to get out.

You see, the new road I committed to taking, could not be raced to the end. It required a slow and steady pace as I was given just enough grace to make it through each day and to the next place.

> If this was the right way, I wondered why it felt so wrong and how long it would be until I reached a new place.

When we find ourselves standing at a crossroad, we often allow our feelings to guide us. But the weight of our feelings changes constantly. We must decide ***not*** to choose our way simply based on feelings. Take control of your decisions and choose the road less traveled. Commit to focusing on your relationship with Christ and leave the heavy weight of your feelings with Him. Commit to becoming the best version of yourself, living your best life, and allowing God to direct your way no matter what or how long it takes. Don't reject the Lord's way – it is the only way that leads to a peaceful place.

> *This is what the Lord says: "Stop at the crossroads and look around. Ask for the old, godly way, and walk in it. Travel its path, and you will find rest for your souls. But you reply, 'No, that's not the road we want!' Jeremiah 6:16 (NLT)*

Day 3

SUFFERING

When we receive blessings that bring us joy, we seldom stop to ask why God blessed us. However, when we go through difficult times it's often our first thought to question why. Why is God allowing me to suffer this way?

We seldom, if ever, stop to consider that oftentimes it is our own will and lack of obedience to God's word that brings us the most suffering. Has God opened this door, or have I run through it ahead of God? When we question what we did to deserve or not deserve our blessings, we are considering that our blessings are in some way a result of our own righteousness or lack thereof, but this is not true.

The Bible tells us that Jacob was a deceitful man prior to his wrestling encounter with God, and yet God still blessed him and his offspring (Genesis 28:13).

However, it is also not wise of us to think that God will bless something that He isn't a part of, and we must be aware that our sin *does* have consequences.

Yes, Jesus died on the cross and paid the price for our sins, but we are given principles to live by to keep us from unnecessary harm. If you are living outside of God's will and instead following your own, this is when the greatest pain and suffering will occur.

For example, if you have given yourself completely to someone outside of marriage and the relationship ends, you have become bound together and it's very difficult to emotionally detach because an ungodly soul tie has been formed. These painful feelings and memories are embedded in our hearts and minds. This is a consequence of sin. But when we are broken and must lean on God to get through our problem this is a blessing in and of itself. There is an intimacy with God that is gained through times of suffering.

While it's difficult to understand how anything positive could come from our broken state this is an opportunity for growth. This is the time to lean into the promises of God, learn from your mistakes, and rise above them. It's so easy to want to give up and turn back to what is comfortable when things don't feel good but if God has called you to surrender something, no matter how difficult it may be, He has a greater purpose for your life and there are blessings to be discovered as you draw near to Him in your suffering.

> *So if you sinful people know how to give good gifts to your children, how much more will your heavenly Father give good gifts to those who ask him. Matthew 7:11 (NLT)*

Day 4

SPIRIT, SOUL, AND BODY

We are made up of our spirit, soul, and body. From the very moment we are saved the spirit of Christ lives within us; we are instantly redeemed. It was long after I became a Christian before I truly grasped that this concept of being **redeemed** meant I was justified or in other words "just-as-if-I'd" never sinned.

Interestingly, even when I had completely grasped it, I still had a hard time accepting it. Although I sometimes struggle with forgiving myself, the truth is God forgives me instantly for everything I ask! However, the sanctification process is *not* instantaneous. Restoring our soul and surrendering our body to conform to and be led by the Spirit within us takes time. But we *are* redeemed! No matter what we have done or what we are going through, God is with us and He loves us. He is merciful, and He gives us all the chances we need to get things right.

When God called me to surrender an unhealthy relationship, while my spirit knew it was the right thing to do, I was having trouble getting my body and soul to submit. I continued to *leave and return* to the relationship. I had to stop depending on myself and instead start asking God to remove the character defects within me that were causing disobedience to Him. I began falling to my knees and crying out to God to comfort me and lead me in the right direction. Every time I wanted to go back, I got on my knees and cried out to God. I told Him when I felt angry, when I felt lonely, when I was hurting and without a doubt, He never failed to meet me there at that moment on my knees.

Along with this journey of healing comes many ups, downs, twists, and turns. There will be days when you feel strong and days you feel weak; days when you feel you have made progress and days you'll feel as if you are back where you started. But one thing you can count on is that the faster you take the next right step the closer you come to the other side. Running back to what is comfortable will not only delay your journey but certainly cause you *additional* pain. Instead, allow your spirit to be your command center rather than your feelings. Run into the arms of your Savior who will rescue you, hold you, and heal you. Your peace will be restored as your body and soul begin to align with your spirit and God's calling on your life.

> *Now may the God of peace make you holy in every way and may your whole spirit and soul and body be kept blameless until our Lord Jesus Christ comes again. 1 Thessalonians 5:23 (NLT)*

Day 5

SPIRIT COMMANDED

There will always be a struggle between our desire to do what's right and our predisposition to do wrong. But we can learn the discipline of hearing the voice of the Spirit and allow it to be our command center rather than our body and soul.

Joyce Meyer once said, "There's nothing more miserable than a born-again sinner." This resonated with me. When my Spirit tells me that I'm operating outside of the will of God, but I persist in doing it anyway, I do feel miserable.

Before embarking upon my personal and spiritual growth and recovery journey, I was that person always trying to convict others of their wrongdoing although knowing that it was not my job but that of the Holy Spirit. My discernment of right and wrong sometimes seemed different from another person. However, I had to recognize that the behavior of others was out of my control and not everyone would have the same discernment of right and wrong nor feel the same misery when functioning outside the will of God.

The Bible says in 1 Corinthians 2:14 (AMP), "But the natural [unbelieving] man does not accept the things [the teachings and revelations] of the Spirit of God, for they are foolishness [absurd and illogical] to him; and he is incapable of understanding them because they are spiritually discerned and appreciated [and he is unqualified to judge spiritual matters]."

We have to learn to forgive and accept people where they are, understanding that we do not wage war against flesh and blood enemies but of evil spirits (Ephesians 6:12). However, at the same time being able to discern our lack of compatibility regarding a relationship is necessary. Jesus paid the price for all of us and the moment we accepted him as our Savior we were made righteous before God and became one with Him through the gift of His Holy Spirit. As you continue to seek God's will for your life, your spirit will become stronger than your body or soul (mind, will, and emotions).

> *I don't really understand myself for I want to do what is right, but I don't do it. Instead, I do what I hate. But if I know that what I am doing is wrong, this shows that I agree that the law is*

good. So I am not the one doing wrong; it is sin living in me that does it. And I know that nothing good lives in me, that is, in my sinful nature. I want to do what is right, but I can't. I want to do what is good, but I don't. I don't want to do what is wrong, but I do it anyway. But if I do what I don't want to do, I am not really the one doing wrong; it is sin living in me that does it.
Romans 7:15- 17 (NLT)

Day 6

YOUR SOUL

Our soul is made up of our *mind*, **will**, and *emotions*. It gives us the ability to think, choose, and express emotions so it's important to understand how easily our choices and emotions can be driven by our thoughts. The *mind* gives us the capacity to think and reason. Our free *will* allows us to make choices. And our *emotions* allow us to have feelings.

Prior to becoming Christians, we discerned right and wrong based upon our own judgment. But when we accept Christ, we become a new person with a desire for our choices and emotions to reflect his Spirit living within us. We are to be vessels operating and living out God's will and His plan for our lives.

I consistently allowed my emotions to cloud my judgment in almost any situation. I reacted based upon my feelings, which of course changed constantly. I was not disciplined to listen to and obey the voice of the Spirit even when I heard it clearly. So many times, I received confirmation that God was asking me to do something, but I allowed my own desires and feelings to drive my actions to do otherwise. As a result, my spirit was never completely at peace. It appeared to always be kicking and screaming until I got to the point where it seemed I couldn't even feel anymore. I was no longer able to sense God's presence in my life. It wasn't that God had left me; it was that I had allowed something else to have greater authority over my life.

For most of us, it takes a lot of discipline and work to keep our emotions in check, but the good news is God will transform our minds as we pursue His will for our lives. Our thoughts can bring us anxiety or bring us peace and prosperity. So, keep your soul (your mind, will, and emotions) in check.

> *Do not conform to the pattern of this world but be transformed by the renewing of your mind. Then you will be able to test and approve what God's will is – his good, pleasing and perfect will.*
> *Romans 12:2 (NIV)*

Day 7

YOUR BODY

In this life, our bodies are temporary homes for our spirit and soul. The Bible refers to our bodies as temples (1 Corinthians 6:19). Before Jesus died on the cross, He said He would send His Comforter. But prior to that time, the only access there was to God was behind the veil in the inner room of the temple called the Holy of Holies. When Jesus died, the veil was ripped open and God's presence moved into the hearts of believers.

As Christians, we need to take pride in our bodies and care for our temple. When we succumb to the desires of our flesh, this opens the door for the enemy to gain a foothold in our lives and we will never be satisfied. That's the thing about sin, you say you're never going to do another line of Oreos, but you find yourself doing it over and over. Is that just me with the Oreos? You are never satisfied because you are looking to satisfy a hunger that can only be satiated by spiritual food. In Matthew 5:6 it says, "Blessed are those who hunger and thirst for righteousness, for they shall be satisfied."

As Christians, we are forgiven for our sins but there are consequences for our sinful actions like the pain we experience. The Bible says we have free will to choose – but some things are not beneficial to us and in fact, enslave us to the power of sin. If you have insisted on having your way and you find yourself caught up in trying to control things that are out of your control, you have allowed these things to take on an inappropriate priority in your life. It's time to surrender.

> *You say, "I am allowed to do anything"- but not everything is good for you. And even though "I am allowed to do anything," I must not become a slave to anything. 1 Corinthian 6:12 (NLT)*

Day 8

APPOINTMENTS

What if I told you right now you have the most important appointment you will ever have with the most significant person in your life, regarding the most vital task you'll ever be called to do? Would you be late for your appointment?

I often pray about something and then open my bible, read a devotional, or talk to someone and there it is - exactly what I needed to hear! I've come to believe things don't happen by chance. As you read this, I believe it is a divine appointment. God has a plan for your life, and the time to begin is now! It's time to let go of what no longer benefits you whether that be fear, a relationship, or any other thing that's holding you back from God's best for your life.

Sometimes the reality of a situation is hard to accept. We see things as they could be and often hold onto that.

Many times, the only thing holding us back is our feelings. Feelings are temporary and ever-changing.

Gaining the abundant blessings God has in store for you requires you to surrender to what He is asking of you and follow where He is leading you regardless of how uncomfortable it may feel. Stepping out of your comfort zone takes discipline, but what awaits *is* worth the discomfort! God has a purpose for your life and it is so much bigger than you. You are being called to rise above. What is God asking you to do?

> *There is an appointed time for everything. And*
> *there is a time for every event under heaven.*
> *Ecclesiastes 3:1 (NASB)*

Day 9

TRUST THE PROCESS

Do you ever feel like your life is spiraling out of control? Then this is the time to put your complete trust in God. He is preparing you for a new journey ahead. Regardless of how it may look or how you may feel He has begun the work in you. Turning back now will not only prolong the process but cause additional pain and suffering. You deserve His best and He has not given up on you.

When you reach the point where you think you can't do it, you're right! Those are the moments you drop to your knees and cry out to the One who can, the One who has complete control over your life...you need only surrender it to Him. Trust in the process of allowing yourself to suffer the unpleasant feelings of loss and withdrawal because it is only then you can overcome them. You are stronger than anything of this world because the Bible tells us that the same Spirit of

Him who raised Jesus from the dead lives in you (Romans 8:11).

I took the following words to heart when my mentor spoke them to me, "The only way to get to the other side of the valley is to walk through it." Keep taking the next right step and you will see God begin to transform your will, your emotions, your soul, and your life! Soon you will look back only to share with others how far the marvelous works of God's hands have brought you.

The time is now. God is asking you to **surrender** those things that He has no part in. You can't trust your ways; you can't understand how to do this, but you can lay it at the feet of Jesus because He knows the way! Let Him take those things from you. Let Him have it. Let go and trust Him to show you His way.

> *Trust in the Lord with all your heart; do not depend on your own understanding. Seek his will in all you do, and he will show you which path to take. Proverbs 3:5-6 (NLT)*

Day 10

DISCIPLINE

When you allow your feelings and emotions to be your command center rather than disciplining yourself to be led by the Holy Spirit you are destined for a life *without* peace. Discipline may seem painful at the moment, but it bears fruit. I can't remember any child ever agreeing to the "art" of discipline, but parents know it's required to lead the child in the right direction. In this same way, our Heavenly Father guides us.

Growing up I always considered observing Lent as something in which only the Catholic Church participated. However, many Christians use this season as a time of discipline and realignment of their hearts. As a season of Lent approached, I knew God was calling me to surrender an unhealthy relationship. What He showed me through that journey was that at the root of this unhealthy relationship was me! My fight to let go was partly a result of the unhealthy relationship I had with *myself*. The negative underlying belief I had of myself caused me to try to overcompensate and left me vulnerable in *other* areas, for example, searching for my worth, love, and acceptance from others. My spirit was left thirsty as I reflected these needs onto my partner, which could only be satiated through my relationship with Christ.

Make *this* your season to feel the pain of discipline. This pain leads to something great versus the pain of choosing your way based on feelings of comfortability. Commit to the hard work of *not* allowing your feelings and emotions to take control; rather, discipline yourself to seek the guidance of the Holy Spirit before you speak or act on anything.

> *No discipline is enjoyable while it is happening –*
> *it's painful! But afterward there will be a peaceful*
> *harvest of right living for those who are trained*
> *this way. Hebrews 12: 11 (NLT)*

Day 11

ACCOUNTABILITY

Our emotions are affected by our feelings which constantly change at any given moment based upon several factors such as simply the amount of sleep we have had or what we did or didn't eat. Making ourselves accountable for our actions before acting upon our feelings will lead to more logical thinking.

Any sedated hospital patient who would otherwise be considered of sound mind to make decisions temporarily refrains from making any legally binding decisions the day of sedation. The sedation, however light, temporarily alters decision-making.

I remember a time I went to the emergency room and was given pain medication. It not only took away the pain, but it impaired my ability to even care about pain temporarily. In this same way, our emotions can interfere with logical decision-making and it's important not to abandon ourselves in the process of dealing with them. Just as the sedated patient needs a trusted individual to drive them safely home, it's important to have an accountability partner during the healing process from an unhealthy relationship to guide you through.

Making the decision to work with a life and recovery coach was one of the best decisions of my life. She guided me but always lovingly reminded me that the choice was mine and a lesson was waiting to be learned behind each decision I made.

Just as God allows me to choose my way and suffer the consequences, I found the same experience held true with my coach. I came to understand that there was wisdom behind her guidance, and it was often a very *painful* experience when I doubted it and chose a different path.

When you find yourself doubting a decision and experiencing the feelings of fear and anxiety that go along with it, reach out to a godly accountability partner who will guide you away from abandoning yourself, your dreams, or your worth based on the temporary and ever-changing feelings you're having at that moment.

Listen to the advice and accept instruction, that you may gain wisdom in the future. Many are the plans in the mind of a man, but it is the purpose of the Lord that will stand. Proverbs 19:20-21 (ESV)

Day 12

WHEN HOPE HURTS

Have you ever had a hopeful vision for your future that was shattered? Did you feel like you failed, like you were alone, or like no one understood? Do you look around at others who seem to be happily living out their hopes and dreams but you are still waiting on yours, or perhaps it seems like yours have just been ripped away?

What have you been hoping for? Maybe it's a significant other, a reconciled relationship, or to have a child.

Whatever it is, placing your hope in something is an emotional investment and when it's misplaced it hurts. The bible tells us that "Hope deferred makes the heart sick" (Proverbs 13:12). If I'm placing all of my hope in people, or relationships, and allowing my happiness to depend on their outcome, when these things don't meet my time frame or my expectations I'm met with heartache and disappointment. Hope that *hurts* leads to a crushed spirit and the bible says "a crushed spirit dries up the bones" (Proverbs 17:22). In other words, it sucks the life right out of you.

The bible tells us, "But if we look forward to something we don't yet have, we must wait patiently and confidently" (Romans 8:25). As you wait expectantly be sure your hope is anchored in Christ. The bible tells us, "This hope is like a firm and steady anchor for our souls" (Hebrews 6:19).

An anchor is used to keep something in place. When we anchor ourselves to the hope found in Christ, this hope keeps us from being tossed around like a ship at sea when storms are closing in around us. The midst of a storm can seem lonely, dark, and dreary. But you are not alone. Others who have gone through or are going through the same thing you are right now. Most importantly God is with you and He knows every hope and every heartache and exactly what they'll bring. The only question is, do you trust Him?

What are the desires of your heart? Do they lead to heartache or hope that hurts? Have you misplaced your hope in treasures of this earth? Hope anchored in Christ brings favor, it sends breakthroughs, and it even restores hope to the hopeless. When our hope is anchored in Christ we can wait with an assurance that this hope is a prosperous one.

Take delight in the Lord and he will give you the desires of your heart. Psalms 37:4 (NIV)

Day 13

DISCERNMENT

hen your spirit is out of alignment with God's calling on your life you will never be completely at peace. It took me a while to learn that my God-given discernment should be trusted. I often required it to be confirmed. I allowed the enemy to plant seeds of doubt and I continued to deny the truth that my spirit revealed. I found myself repeatedly asking the Lord for confirmations.

I realized that I never prayed a single prayer asking God whether He was leading me into a relationship I chose, yet there I was continuously praying for confirmation that I should get out. This ultimately ended in a lesson that requiring my discernment to be proven can be a painful experience. I ignored and endured many more months of the same and worse, before *finally* walking away very wounded.

Allow the Holy Spirit to be your command center and this will bring you peace that surpasses all understanding. This is not to say the journey isn't difficult; in fact, oftentimes things can feel worse before they feel better. But when you keep your focus on the fact that on the other side of this journey is the resurrection power that changes lives, you can be certain that as a Christian you are anointed, and that anointing gives you the power to do what God has called you to do.

Do you trust in your spiritual discernment or do you require it to be proven? Sometimes when we repeatedly fail to listen to God's voice, our sense of spiritual connection can feel broken. We put ourselves in a position that causes our disobedience to separate us from hearing God's voice. God will be faithful to bring darkness to light as we trust in Him and heed His warnings.

> *But you have received the Holy Spirit, and he lives within you, so you don't need anyone to teach you what is true. For the Spirit teaches you everything you need to know, and what he teaches is true – it is not a lie. So just as he has taught you, remain in fellowship with Christ.*
> *1 John 2:27 (NLT)*

Day 14

GRIEVING

There are several stages to grief, and they don't always come in order, but eventually the final stage of acceptance arrives – and with it comes healing.

While the grieving process is different for everyone, when we suffer a loss we all grieve in some way. The grieving process after the loss of my mom, my divorce, the end of my first relationship after divorce, and so on were all very different. I recycled through different stages several times before the healing came.

The grieving process can be intense, and our emotions can become erratic. Upon ending an unhealthy relationship, I saw myself in a state of *Denial* many times. I didn't completely believe it had to be the end of the relationship and I kept hoping for change.

When I wasn't in denial about things, I felt *Anger*. I was angry with myself, my partner, and sometimes any random person that happened to cross my path during that time.

I often found myself stuck in the *Bargaining* stage. I constantly re-played everything in my head and analyzed every situation obsessively until finally becoming intentional in giving up my desire to control the outcome. I sensed a deep sadness, many refer to it as the stage of *Depression*, as I felt the hurt and loss of realizing that I couldn't change things and had to move forward. This was followed by *Acceptance*. This was when my new normal began to arrive along with the peace that came from living in the present and having a better vision for my future.

As you cycle through the grieving process there will be many twists and turns – so don't think you'll never find peace and acceptance if, for example, you've gone from anger back to denial. The truth is, we can't change the situation, but we can grieve it and move on as a healed, whole, and complete person. You may *feel* alone for a season, but in reality, you are never alone. God is always with you and watching over you.

> *The Lord is near to the heartbroken and He saves those who are crushed in spirit (contrite in heart, truly sorry for their sin). Psalms 34:18 (AMP)*

Day 15

PURSUED

Many times, we say we want to do God's will and not our own, yet we continue to do the very things that are not in alignment with this. However, if you have temporarily lost sight of pursuing God and His will for your life, God is always faithful to continue His pursuit of you.

We can be confident in knowing that God never stops pursuing his children or calling us back when we start to veer from the plans that He has for us. I'm so thankful He doesn't give up on me. He is always faithful to give me as many chances as I need to get things right.

During the times I didn't feel God's nearness in my life it wasn't that He left me; rather, it was the all-consuming distractions that I allowed to silence Him. Not only did God never leave me but He pursued me relentlessly.

Several times, I prayed for confirmations and was given blatantly obvious signs, yet still, I doubted. I remember in one situation asking for just one more confirmation and God was faithful to provide it, yet months went by before I finally surrendered. Without fail, God was faithful to continuously pursue me and show me, in one way or another, those things that were not a part of His plan for my future.

If you have been distracted for a time and made decisions that were not part of God's will for your life, remember He uses all things for our good when we are called according to His purpose (Romans 8:28). As you pursue God's purpose for your life, He will use you in amazing ways.

Surely your goodness and unfailing love will pursue me all the days of my life, and I will live in the house of the Lord forever. Psalms 23:6 (NLT)

Day 16

ATTRACTION

When you recognize yourself in a pattern of unhealthy relationships, it's time to stop blaming the other person and look inward to see where the problem lies within you.

Nobody intentionally seeks out an unhealthy relationship. Yet somehow, that's where I found myself on more than one occasion. Most of us have heard the saying that you don't attract what you want; you attract what you are. I thought there was something wrong with everyone else and I couldn't possibly be a part of the problem. But God began to reveal that it wasn't "they're all the same" or "there are no more good ones out there."

The common denominator in each of my unhealthy relationships was me! The people I chose to engage with were often a reflection of myself. How could I possibly have attracted the healthy, whole, spiritual leader I desired, one impressed more by my walk with God than my physical beauty if I was not living this life? God said when a man and a woman join, two become one. In my broken state, I was unintentionally attracting another "broken half" to complete me, but this is not how God designed us to be.

> I thought there was something wrong with everyone else and I couldn't possibly be a part of the problem.

God never asks us to surrender something to Him without having something far better in store for us. But we must allow Him to remove the taste for those things that are not good for us. We must seek God first and be made whole in Him before we can have a healthy relationship the way He designed it to be.

> *Then Christ will make his home in your hearts as you trust in him. Your roots will grow down into God's love and keep you strong. And may you have the power to understand, as all God's people should, how wide, how long, how high, and how deep his love is. May you experience the love of Christ, though it is too great to understand fully. Then you will be made complete with all the fullness of life and power that comes from God.*
> *Ephesians 3:17-21 (NLT)*

Day 17

GROWTH

When we are headed in the direction of growth – fear and anxiety often creep in to stop us in our tracks and cause us to turn back where things are familiar and comfortable.

I heard one of my favorite motivational speakers, Terri Savelle Foy, say that the words, "May you stay in one place forever" were once used as a curse against an enemy. She went on to talk about the bible story of Lot and his wife. In this Bible story, they were told to leave the city and not look back.

The moment Lot's wife looked back she was met with her destiny – she was destroyed. This is a great motivator to be driven forward and to stop looking back, worrying about the past and the things that didn't work out as planned or the things that you didn't do right.

Your destiny is certainly not behind you! Your future lies ahead of you! Be mindful of what God is calling you to leave in the past. Do not look back. Instead, focus on what He is calling you toward now. Then go ahead and let those feelings of fear and anxiety sit with you for a while if necessary, but never allow these to cause you to turn back to what is familiar and comfortable because there is no growth there. In fact, staying in one place forever could be considered a curse!

Always trust that if God called you *to* it, He will see you *through* it because He doesn't *call* the qualified, He *qualifies* the called! He equips us with whatever we need to fulfill what he has called us to do. Where is your destiny? What are you being called to do?

> *I'm not saying that I have this all together, that I have it made. But I am well on my way, reaching out for Christ, who has so wondrously reached out for me. Friends don't get me wrong: By no means do I count myself an expert in all of this, but I've got my eye on the goal, where God is beckoning us onward—to Jesus. I'm off and running, and I'm not turning back. Philippians 3:13 (MSG)*

Day 18

PRUNING

For everything, there is a season and a reason, but when it's time for a change, God will ask us to surrender things that are no longer serving us and His plan for our lives.

As I've reflected on different seasons of my life, I'm reminded time and again that God is forever trying to prune things from it that are not life-giving. God always has a way of reminding me that His plans are far superior to my own. To grow and become the person God has called me to be, I must step out in faith rather than staying where things are comfortable. It's no easy task but the reward is great!

I love the story of the little girl with the pearl necklace. She adored her faux pearl necklace that her mommy bought her. She wore them everywhere and they made her feel so special. One evening as she was getting ready for bed her daddy asked her if she loved him. The little girl loved her daddy very much but when he asked her to give him her pearls, she insisted that he could have *anything else*, but she didn't want to give up her pearls.

Her daddy assured her that he still loved her even though she couldn't give up her pearls. This happened several nights until one night with trembling lips the little girl opened her hand and placed her pearls in her daddy's hand. As she did, from his other hand her daddy pulled out of his pocket a strand of genuine pearls. He had been waiting for her to give up the dime-store pearls so he could give her something far better.

Our Heavenly Father is patiently waiting. It's hard to hand over something that we have become so attached to, especially when we can't see what's in the other hand. But through the pruning process, you can be certain that God has something so much greater in store for you.

> *"Every branch in Me that does not bear fruit, He takes away; and every branch that continues to bear fruit, He [repeatedly] prunes, so that it will bear more fruit [even richer and finer fruit]."*
> John 15:2 (AMP)

Day 19

DOUBT

When doubt creeps in it can stop us in our tracks. We must discipline ourselves to hear and listen to the nudges of our spirit. Don't doubt that even when you can't see it or feel it, God is still working.

A little over six months had passed since I stopped sharing most of my growth journey publicly when I began to hear a calling to do more. Shortly after, I began receiving confirmations of this beginning when a woman reached out to me saying she was going through a difficult time and asked me to pray for her. She told me that when she was asked who she would contact during a difficult or dark place she told them it was me. I thought to myself, "why me?" How was I qualified to be this person to anyone? It was that voice of doubt again. I discovered that she had been following my journey and was encouraged.

It wasn't easy to share my difficult moments publicly while at the same time trying to be encouraging and inspiring to others. But I learned that it wasn't necessary to have overcome this "thing," that even during the midst of it all I was uniquely qualified to speak to others and inspire them through my journey. There were very few that seemed to engage or support me, most sat quietly on the side; however, they were there, and they were listening.

I found a quote that said, "Start where you are, use what you have, do what you can." That's it! We don't have to be on the other side of the storm. We can start where we are right now and use what we are going through to inspire and encourage someone else. We can continue taking the next right step and allow God to do the rest.

> *Jesus immediately reached out his hand and took hold of him, saying to him, "O you of little faith, why did you doubt?" Matthew 14:31 (ESV)*

Day 20

GAINS AND LOSSES

*L*etting go and realizing a loss can feel devastating. But, it's only once this is underway that you can begin to see glimpses of the unrealized gains that await you.

Working in the field of accounting, I'm exposed to gains and losses in financial records. This prompted me to reflect on how investors who hold securities in a company can determine their gain or loss by comparing the value at two different points in time. However, until these investors let go of that security or in other words sell it, the gain or loss has no realized value because there is no exchange of cash.

When a stock is performing well, and its future looks promising it can be considered a wise decision to hold onto it as you see growth. But when performing poorly, while some investors jump ship at the first sign of a loss and invest elsewhere because it's no longer benefiting them to stay in that stock, others hold on until they suffer significant losses out of hope that the stocks' future will change for the better. When there is no indication of future growth, and history shows unfavorable losses, it's unwise not to take measures to protect yourself from suffering an irreparable loss.

The same holds true when it comes to our relationships. We need to assess the risk and return on our investment. When God brings two people together there will be signs of a promising future, a spiritual and emotional intimacy, and a peace that indicates it's a safe place to invest your time and future. However, when there is no indication of growth and your peace has all but disappeared, it's not wise to simply hope that the future of this relationship will be different when history has already shown it to the contrary.

The safe thing to do is realize your loss and invest elsewhere. Please understand that if you are married, I'm not advocating divorce. However, if you are married and this resonates with you, it may be time to invest in future growth prior to suffering a significant loss.

You can't receive or realize what God has in store for you until you let go of what's not benefiting you. Don't allow the fear of suffering loss or having to start over, prevent you from realizing the gain that God has in store. So, what type of investor are you?

But whatever were gains to me I now consider loss for the sake of Christ. What is more, I consider everything a loss because of the surpassing worth of knowing Christ Jesus my Lord, for whose sake I have lost all things. I consider them garbage, that I may gain Christ. Philippians 3:7-8 (NIV)

Day 21

TRAUMA BOND

Many times, I found myself questioning if things were *that* bad in my relationship with someone. But, through lies and betrayal, I had lost the respect I should have in a partner and found myself thinking that I no longer even really liked this person. Yet, I could not detach. My mind and body longed for him. I was experiencing classic signs of a betrayal trauma bond.

When I first learned of trauma bonds it was somewhat of a relief. I finally had some answers as to why it was so difficult to break free from the toxic relationship that I was in.

According to research done by Patrick Carnes, PhD., the excitement and intensity of this kind of relationship are mistaken for love when it's really a form of addiction. Regrettably, my brain became addicted to the chemical and emotional cycle of abuse. During a low point, I felt the only thing that could make me feel better was affection from this person – but when I got this "fix" and experienced the "high," it was just temporary, and the cycle repeated.

It was difficult for me to recognize my relationship as emotionally abusive because of the "love bombing" that was intertwined. Similar to overcoming drug addiction, I went through withdrawals and relapses. I relapsed many times going back into the toxic relationship, even after deciding to leave.

I had to overcome my denial about the relationship and make a daily decision not to give in to the temptation of getting that "fix." I realized as with any other addiction, the chance of relapse was very high, and the only way I could reduce it was to **eliminate all contact**. It seemed scary at first and the withdrawal symptoms I felt were real! But I had to stop diminishing what I had gone through by remembering only the good times or questioning if things were that bad. I *finally* surrendered my desire to control the situation and I leaned into my faith.

> I found myself thinking that I no longer even really liked this person. Yet, I could not detach. My mind and body longed for him.

Although trauma bonds are extremely difficult and painful to break, healing is possible. The temporary relief from reaching out never lasts and it does more harm in the process. Are you ready to discipline yourself to make decisions based on what is in your *best interest* rather than your *feelings and emotions*?

Have faith that as you focus on one day at a time, and until you have a healthier mindset to reevaluate the situation, God will bring healing.

> *There is a way that seems right to a man, but its end is the way to death. Proverbs 14:12 (ESV)*

Day 22

TRUST

Even the unhealthiest relationship can be tempting to stay in when you are unhealthy yourself. When you come to a place wherein you feel too weak to keep moving forward – rather than giving in to your feelings and turning back, drop to your knees and trust in the One who will hold you and heal you.

Early on in my recovery from an unhealthy relationship, I set a specific daily prayer time on my calendar and each evening I would use this time to be on my knees in prayer. While I also prayed little prayers throughout the day, I knew this special time on my knees together with the Lord was healing me, so much so that I sometimes ran to my prayer spot and dropped to my knees hours before the scheduled time. This is how I would overcome the daily temptation to open the door to that unhealthy place again.

When we get to a point that our emotions seem to be all over the place, we can trust in God to be our strength and our provider. He will always meet us where we are and provide what we need in each moment.

I remember the new friends God brought me during this difficult time in my life. One evening, after another rough day, as I made my way to my prayer spot, one of these new friends sent me a song. Because I usually listen to a song before and sometimes during my praying, I started listening to it. I remember crying and I wrote these words in my journal: "…dare to believe how much God loves me."

God has a plan for your life, and He will give you the tools you need to fulfill that plan. He understands and has compassion towards you. Wherever you have been, He has been also. Although you are weak and tempted, God is there to provide for your every need in each moment. Spend the extra time in prayer and bible reading and watch God begin to transform your life. When we completely put our trust in God and understand that while we can't trust in ourselves to fix things, if we ask Him, He will begin to remove the taste for things that are not good for us.

For we do not have a high priest who is unable to empathize with our weakness, but we have one who has been tempted in every way, just as we are

– yet he did not sin. Let us then approach God's throne of grace with confidence so that we may receive mercy and find grace to help us in our time of need. Hebrews 4:15 (NIV)

Here's a song I'd like to share with you – Dancing on the Waves:
https://youtu.be/nWmjpF613y4

Day 23

LESSONS

*I*n nearly every situation of life, a lesson can be learned whether good or bad. When we face what feels like a failure, we can choose a grateful attitude and keep moving forward.

For a very long time, I had a false belief that the actions and reactions of others toward me were a reflection of myself and my worth. However, through my personal and spiritual growth and recovery journey, I finally grasped the concept that the actions of others are their own and we cannot take them upon ourselves.

I began to see every situation in a new way and look for the lesson to carry with me. I began to feel a sense of sorrow for the people who hurt or betrayed me, and an understanding that they are broken, as are we all. Through my journey to healing, I had to accept that sometimes people will only be in our lives for a season. But in every season, we can find a lesson, even if it's just a lesson to carry with us to protect us in the future. God can transform your thoughts and show you how to let go of resentment as He heals you and changes your heart toward others.

As crazy as it sounds, I truly reached the point of counting it a blessing to have experienced many of life's difficulties. This wasn't always my attitude, but I've come to understand that without these trials I would not have the relationship I have with Christ today.

It's in those seasons of life that I truly had to depend on God, I experienced His presence and knew He was with me. With the right mindset, there comes a point in time when we have the perspective that difficulties lead to growth. A point when you can see the good and the bad in nearly every situation. We can look back with wisdom as we allow God to use the trials we face to bring us closer to Him and become a better version of ourselves.

> *Consider it pure joy, my brothers and sisters, whenever you face trials of many kinds, because you know that the testing of your faith produces perseverance. Let perseverance finish its work so that you may be mature and complete, not lacking anything. James 1: 2-4 (NIV)*

Day 24

GET UP

As I prayed for God to heal what was broken in me, I realized I had to be willing to take the first steps. I had to rise to the occasion, pick up my mat, and walk. In the bible story about the invalid man at the pool in Jerusalem, when Jesus saw the man had been there for 38 years, He asked him if he wanted to get well. The invalid man was so focused on what he couldn't do for himself that he didn't even respond with a "yes." Still, Jesus healed him.

So many times, we are so focused on where we are, our problems, and our failures, it can feel like we are trying to accomplish the impossible. We decide to surrender something, but circle back around and repeat the process.

Why did God tell the man to pick up his mat? If the man had been there 38 years with the same mat it couldn't have been of any value or worth caring for, right? Well, if you stay somewhere for 38 years you must be comfortable there – whether it's enjoyable or not.

God was asking the man to leave his comfort zone. Not only did this new journey require leaving his comfort zone and continuing to walk in the right direction, but it required leaving *nothing* behind including his old mat!

In this same way, God sometimes asks us to cut ties with our past, and "picking up our mat" means leaving nothing behind but our old ways. God also may be asking you to leave your comfort zone and pick up your music and go sing, or pick up your bible and go teach. Whatever it is God is asking you to do, embrace it with faith.

Even though at times we are not our best, God is working through us and for us. It's up to us to choose whether we will listen when God speaks, just as the invalid man did and was healed – or whether we continue the fight to hold onto what feels comfortable and familiar. Do you want to be healed?

> *Then Jesus said to him, "Get up! Pick up your mat and walk." At once the man was cured; he picked up his mat and walked...*
> John 5: 8-9 (NIV)

Day 25

FEELING STUCK

I attended a talk show called "Recovery's Got Talent." Not only was the talent amazing, but to hear what God had done to change the lives of these talented people was incredible.

At first, all I could think of was how wonderful it would be if someone very close to me, who was struggling with drug addiction, could hear these messages and find hope. I continued to pray for that person's healing while I also began to focus on my own recovery. Although I never struggled with drugs or alcohol, the hope that one day I, too, would overcome what I was battling was encouraging.

At the time, it never crossed my mind that I could inspire hope in others by what I had been through just as these amazing recovery stories were inspiring me and so many others away from staying stuck in pain.

When I felt like I was stuck and didn't have the strength to take the next right step, I did something different: I waited. I waited upon the Lord. The key to getting "unstuck" lies in understanding that God can transform our way of thinking. It may not happen overnight, but neither does our pattern of negative thinking.

From the time we are born our brains begin adapting to repeated patterns until it becomes a natural process. This same process is how I knew I could overcome anything. I often think back to the days right after my mom passed away. When I woke up in the morning, she was my first thought, the last at night, and she was on my mind throughout the day. But as I went about life, engaging in other activities and changing the repeated pattern of calling her every day, my brain began adapting to this new way of life, and eventually, it was as much a habit not to think of calling her.

Have you felt discouraged by your progress? Do you sometimes feel like you've been stuck in the same spot for a while? Ask the Lord to meet you where you are and be confident that He will lead you to the next right step.

> *I would have despaired had I not believed that I would see the goodness of the Lord in the land of the living. Wait for and confidently expect the Lord; Be strong and let your heart take courage; Yes, wait for and confidently expect the Lord.*
> *Psalms 27:13-14 (AMP)*

Day 26

SELF-WORTH

Aren't you amazed at God's thoughts of you? He planned every detail of your being and before anyone else ever knew of you, He had your whole life planned out. You are wonderfully made and worthy of His best.

A while back, I read a short little story from an unknown author about self-worth and I loved it. I customized it slightly to be more fitting to me and listed these qualities below.

- Striving for excellence spiritually because God does not want me to be unequally yoked.
- A high level of integrity in dealing with relationships because lies and are not part of a godly person.
- Someone I can respect because God knows I won't be submissive to a person who is not worthy of my respect.

- Striving for excellence mentally because God knows I enjoy conversation and mental stimulation.
- Striving for excellence financially because God wants us to be good stewards of our finances.
- Family-oriented, a leader and provider to the lives we are entrusted by God
- Sensitive enough to understand me and strong enough to keep me grounded.
- Laughter - because I love to laugh and a merry heart does good, like medicine.

When you believe in the depths of your soul that you are worthy, everything begins to change. Let this be a reminder that *you are worthy* of God's best. Wait on it and expect it! In the meantime, enjoy where you are in each moment. Have faith that God will bring what is meant for you, to you. I invite you to list the qualities you admire in yourself or even those that you strive for, and those that you look for in others.

You made all the delicate inner parts of my body and knit me together in my mother's womb. Thank you for making me so wonderfully complex! Your workmanship is marvelous-how well I know it. You watched me as I was being formed in utter seclusion, as I was woven together in the dark of the womb. You saw me before I was

born. Every day of my life was recorded in your book. Every moment was laid out before a single day had passed. How precious are your thoughts about me Oh God. They cannot be numbered!"
Psalms 139:13-17 (NLT)

Day 27

PROGRESS NOT PERFECTION

I don't know about you, but I'm the type of person who wants to see immediate results. As I began my journey to find healing, I felt like I was slow to make progress and it was *frustrating* at times. I continued to practice the principles that exemplified my new self, but there were some things that I just continued to struggle with. But it was in those honest moments on my knees with God, confessing that I had messed up again and asking Him to remove these character defects that did not embody living a life according to His will, that He began to change me.

As I began to speak to others about my journey, I remember on one occasion feeling attacked by someone as they questioned my growth when I didn't do things perfectly as they would see it. Honestly, I often attacked myself when I didn't do things perfectly. Ultimately, my journey was never about what I was doing *perfectly*, but what God was doing in *and* through me. What I've learned is that we must allow ourselves mistakes because they're going to happen. Acceptance that we will never do everything perfectly brings a sense of peace and understanding that no matter how many times we mess up, the important thing is that we have made progress. In fact, sometimes there is progress in simply recognizing that we messed up!

I want you to know that you are not a finished project. God is still working on you and He will be there to give you another opportunity to get things right every time you ask. So, stand strong, know you're not alone in your weaknesses, and remember not only that someone else may be watching and being inspired by your journey, but it's about progress, not perfection.

Christ is made perfect in our weakness. The only reason you are not perfect is that God is not done with you yet. I don't know about you, but I'm ok with that. I don't ever want God to be done with me. So, I've learned to do something new and instead of trying to change myself, I let God do the work. Continue to practice the principles that exemplify your new self and allow God to control the rest.

But he said to me, "My grace is sufficient for you, for my power is made perfect in weakness." Therefore I will boast all the more gladly about my weaknesses, so that Christ's power may rest on me. 2 Corinthians 12:9 (NIV)

Day 28

YOUR ASSIGNMENT

*I*n the first chapter of the book of Jeremiah we are told that before God formed Jeremiah, He appointed him for a specific assignment as a prophet to all the nations. Jeremiah questioned his ability and alleged he did not know how to speak. But the Lord said, "Behold (hear me), I have put My words in your mouth" (Jeremiah 1:9 AMP).

How many times has God called you to an assignment, but you allowed your doubt and insecurity to interfere? God assured Jeremiah that everywhere He sent him and whatever He commanded him to do, He would be there with him. Be confident in knowing that you are uniquely qualified to carry out the assignment God has given you.

For some of us, this is much easier said than done. God gave me a gift of singing, but my initial experience of fear in doing so followed me. Even winning a national singing competition with my best friend at sixteen years old was no match for my insecurity. No matter how many times I got on stage, I expected that initial experience of nervousness and fear, and it was always sure to show up in one way or another. I walked away from singing for many years. But that didn't mean it wasn't an assignment that God gave me. It meant that I was choosing not to fulfill the assignment He gave me.

One day, when you answer God as to whether you completed the assignment that He gave you, what will your answer be? Do you think He doesn't know who you are or that He could have possibly chosen the wrong person for the assignment He gave you?

God says "Before I formed you in the womb, I knew you [and approved of you as My chosen instrument] . . ." (Jeremiah 1:5 AMP). Is it possible that God gave you an assignment based upon what you've been through so that you could help others? What about the gifts and talents God has given you? Are you using them to glorify him? Whatever the case, you have an assignment that only you can complete. What is God calling you to do?

> *But the Lord said to me, "Do not say, 'I am too young.' You must go to everyone I send you to and say whatever I command you. Do not be afraid for them, for I am with you and will rescue you," declares the Lord. Jeremiah 1:7-8 (NIV)*

Day 29

LONELINESS

We all experience feelings of loneliness after a loss. Sometimes that's exactly what is required to "get yourself together." Growth awaits in the temporary feelings of loneliness.

As I began the journey of healing from the past, I couldn't understand if this was the right thing to do, why was it so difficult? I couldn't see an end to the suffering, and I felt like I needed a way out.

I'm a deadline-oriented person and when no one could give me a specific time frame as to how long I would have to endure the suffering, I had to give up trying to control the timing and depend on God to get me through it.

The Bible tells us the prophet Jeremiah cried out to God reciting all that he had done for Him and then questioned God's promise to help him and protect him. He refers to his loneliness and suffering as an incurable wound. In Jeremiah 15:19 (NLT) it says, "This is how the Lord responds: 'If you return to me, I will restore you so you can continue to serve me. If you speak good words rather than worthless ones you will be my spokesman. You must influence them; do not let them influence you!"

It's better to choose temporary feelings of loneliness than misery that loves company. When we return to God and put our trust in Him, He restores us. Allow yourself to suffer the unpleasant feelings of loss and withdrawal for it is only then that you will begin to see God working. You will experience God transforming your will, your emotions, your soul, and your life!

I'll never forget the day I realized there was hope in overcoming a particular struggle I was facing. I felt as though I had made it to the middle of the valley and the journey to the other side was in sight. For the first time, I was able to see where I had been and know that there was a day approaching when I would confidently say I no longer wanted or needed those things in my life that were not good for me.

It's sometimes difficult to trust God amidst our circumstances. But Jeremiah continued to follow the calling God placed on him and as a result, he went on to declare how blessed he was.

But blessed are those who trust in the Lord and have made the Lord their hope and confidence. They are like trees planted along a riverbank, with roots that reach deep into the water. Such trees are not bothered by the heat or worried by long months of drought. Their leaves stay green, and they never stop producing fruit.
Jeremiah 17: 7-8 (NLT)

Day 30

THE JOURNEY

As I committed to taking a journey of disciplining and realigning my heart, I quickly realized that my spirit had been out of alignment with God's calling on my life and I had lost the peace that is promised to me as a Christian.

When I first began sharing pieces of my journey publicly, I hid for the most part how difficult the journey had been for me. In fact, I remember saying that sometimes things can get worse before getting better – and this held to be true. Shortly into it, I came face to face again with this unhealthy relationship standing at my door, literally. There were many times this won back my attention and affection, but one time was all it took to start the ball in motion to stay the course and do the hard work of kicking that former way of reacting to situations based on feelings and emotions to the curb. And, guess what? I found power and freedom there!

> I quickly realized that my spirit had been out of alignment with God's calling on my life and I had lost the peace that is promised to me as a Christian.

Still, the days ahead were a struggle. But I called in reinforcements by way of prayer and a trusted advisor full of wisdom. I also refocused myself daily on the complete freedom that awaited me on the other side of this journey. Today, I can celebrate that I'm in a better place emotionally and spiritually. Make no mistake, it was certainly not by my doing but the power of God in my life. Being on my knees in prayer every single day and the more intimate relationship I found with Christ has been and always will be the ultimate game-changer.

If you are anything like me, music speaks as nothing else can. During my journey, I found a song that led me through some tough times. It went along so perfectly with the words of my original commitment to my journey that I felt they were taken straight from my mouth. That song is "Spirit Lead Me" by Michael Ketterer & Influence Music. I pray that you are encouraged to recognize unhealthy relationships in your life, whether it be drugs, alcohol, food, people, or anything else, and know that there is a higher power that will lead you to freedom. You need only to ask and believe.

And I will give you a new heart, and I will put a new spirit in you. I will take out your stony, stubborn heart and give you a tender, responsive heart. And I will put my Spirit in you so that you will follow my decrees and be careful to obey my regulations. Ezekiel 36: 26-27 (NLT)

Here's the song I'd like to share with you: Spirit Lead Me – https://youtu.be/ABWnLjXer10

Day 31

RETRAIN YOUR BRAIN

Our subconscious mind stores our beliefs about ourselves, so when you are subconsciously stuck in a negative thought pattern, this could influence your way of handling the present moment.

If you've ever witnessed a toddler throwing a tantrum, you know how unsuccessful they are at controlling their emotions. They "feel" that they must have that very thing they want at that very moment. But the mother is careful to discern what is best for her child not solely based upon feelings; so, she redirects the child's focus away from potentially unhealthy or harmful things to something better. While it can sometimes seem that there is a temporary loss of sanity for both the mother and child, it's just temporary. Eventually, the child goes about their business, learning from these repeated experiences how to better handle their feelings and emotions in the future.

Here's an excellent strategy: Challenge yourself to consider what the best version of yourself would do in a particular situation and begin to retrain your brain. That simple yet powerful goal allowed me to begin profoundly changing my subconscious beliefs. The voice that was so often harsh, critical, doubtful, and which usually corresponded with my feelings at that moment, was replaced with one of love and wisdom similar to the mother who encourages and corrects her child.

As adults, we sometimes never reach our full potential because we allow ourselves to focus on, and give into, what is comfortable or makes us feel better in the moment. The more often this happens, the longer it takes to see our God-given potential. When we learn to love ourselves unconditionally, as a mother does her child, and retrain our brain to redirect our focus, we become closer to reaching our best self.

> *Do not be conformed to this world, but be transformed by the renewal of your mind, that by testing you may discern what is the will of God, what is good and acceptable and perfect.*
> *Romans 12:2 (ESV)*

Day 32

FINDING JOY

At the end of the day, we are not only responsible for our actions but also finding joy *despite* our circumstances. It's easy to cling to familiar things. And letting go of those things that not only do not benefit us but can be detrimental to our spirit, soul, and body – is often extremely difficult. This is often very challenging because we are looking for exterior things to fulfill our happiness.

There was a point in time when I unknowingly looked to other people for happiness, specifically an intimate relationship. Even when I was involved with someone whom I knew I would never marry, I still found it extremely difficult to let go because I was trying to find my happiness there.

To choose wisely in dating and letting go, I had to learn to find my joy from within, in spite of any circumstance. When you reach the point that you are a happy and whole individual, it is at that point wherein you have something great to offer someone else and you choose not to settle for less-than-the-same.

I've been through some things in this lifetime that I could never have made it through without my faith. When my spirit, soul, and body are in alignment with God's Truth, no circumstance can alter my joy because I know the Creator of this universe is always working things out for the good of those who love Him and are called according to His purpose.

It's important to pay attention to the second part of that verse. If you are not walking out God's purpose for your life, then you must not expect everything to work out for your good. So, leave behind what doesn't benefit you, set your mind on the things of the future, and ask God to reveal what needs to be addressed in your life to fit the "and called according to His purpose."

> *And we know that God causes everything to work together for the good of those who love God and are called according to his purpose for them.*
> *Romans 8:28 (NLT)*

Day 33

SELF-AWARENESS

Although sometimes difficult, we must learn to sit with our emotions, accept what we're feeling, and understand why we are feeling it. Sometimes we don't know what we don't know until we know it, right? What I know now is that so many times, people just don't have the tools they need to cope with their feelings and emotions that surround a situation. So, unhealthy relationships can become a crutch – whether it be with food, drugs, alcohol, people, or something else.

I have always been a fairly emotional person and I often apologized for it. When I was sad, I tried to hold back tears, and when angry I felt bad about it. While there are situations where an apology is warranted due to our inappropriate reactions, our emotions need no apology. In sadness, we can look to God for healing, and in anger, for His wisdom. We can feel our emotions then give them to God and carry on in peace.

Learning to sit with our emotions, sense what we're feeling, and recognize why doesn't mean we allow these feelings and emotions to control us or influence our decision-making. It's just the opposite. We are to evaluate ourselves to see if we are living in faith (2 Corinthians 13:5). When we learn not to run from or try to suppress our feelings and emotions, this amazing thing happens – we develop self-awareness!

When we acknowledge our emotions of sadness, anger, disappointment, and others, we can reflect on the event that caused these feelings and begin to invite God in, to teach us how to manage them in a healthy, spiritual way.

> *Pay close attention to yourself [concentrate on your personal development] and to your teaching; persevere in these things [hold to them], for as you do this you will ensure salvation for yourself and for those who hear you. 1 Timothy 4:16 (AMP)*

Day 34

TRANSFORMATION

When we grasp the understanding that God has given us His Spirit which has the power to reign over our will and emotions our lives can be *completely transformed*. Change takes time, consistency, and a lot of hard work! Did I say it takes a lot of hard work? It takes a tremendous amount of hard work. But the beauty here is that while we are trying to do all the hard work to create change, God is there waiting for us to surrender it to Him. When we put our focus on God and allow Him to begin the transformation process in our lives, this is where the ***real*** work takes place.

For me, letting people see my imperfections was a failure, and failure was never an acceptable option. For most of my life, I worked very hard trying to achieve ***perfection***. So, when I began to share some of my journey publicly to hold myself accountable for staying in the race, it became more difficult as I began to feel dangerously close to exposing some of the most vulnerable details of my "failures." But I believed it was what God had called me to do and I trusted that He would use it to encourage someone else in their journey and begin a transformation in their life. What I wasn't aware of was how much it would benefit *me* and completely transform me in the process.

Sometimes I felt angry and resentful that I allowed myself to get into such unhealthy relationships that it began to change who I was. Actually, I wasn't sure at the time that I ever even knew who I was. I certainly didn't feel worthy of God's best. I was trying to fill an empty void within myself with an intimate relationship. I never understood why surrendering an unhealthy relationship was such a painful experience for me until I began the recovery process that allowed me to understand things I could have never understood otherwise. It also brought healing that I wasn't even aware I needed.

Harboring unforgiveness and holding onto resentment will keep you stuck in your emotions but surrendering these to the Lord and allowing him to work results in ***true transformation***.

> *And we all, who with unveiled faces contemplate the Lord's glory, are being transformed into his image with ever-increasing glory, which comes from the Lord, who is the Spirit. 2 Corinthians 3:18 (NIV)*

Day 35

PLANT YOURSELF

Gardeners know that the texture of soil helps determine how it will react under different conditions. Choosing the best soil sets up the most favorable foundation for growth. The same can be said of us. In the same way a Gardener plans out his garden, selectively chooses the seeds, and tends to pruning what is preventing growth, God has planned our lives, chosen us for a specific purpose, and tends to us, pruning what surrounds us that is no longer life-giving.

We tend to try to plan things according to *our* will, and we often fight the pruning process that allows us to grow into who God has created us to be. When we find ourselves reacting inappropriately under certain conditions, we can't expect to stay planted in the same place but yield a different result. Just as important as the soil is to the growth of plants, we are influenced by the people we choose to surround ourselves with.

In gardening, there is a term called "forcing" that encourages a bulb to grow out of season. This method creates an environment that tricks the plant into thinking it is the right season for growth no matter what season it may be. Are you planted so deeply in something that God has been trying to prune from your life that you can't grow without some major "forcing"? When you allow the pruning process to take place, plant yourself in God's word and what He is calling you to do, then you will begin to flourish and bear fruit.

> *But the godly will flourish like palm trees and grow strong like the cedars of Lebanon. For they are transplanted to the Lord's own house. They flourish in the courts of our God. Even in old age they will still produce fruit; they will remain vital and green. Psalms 92:12-14*

Day 36

BE AN INFLUENCE

veryone can be influenced, and everyone can be an influence. In fact, we were made to be an influence and let our light shine.
I remember back to my first pregnancy. My mom asked me if I was sure I was pregnant because at almost five months along there were still no significant signs of my belly growing. However, not too long after, she began to see some change happening and by the time I was a couple of months farther along no one could question the change. This is the same way we grow in Christ. We are immediately redeemed when we accept Christ, but the sanctification process is not as immediate. However, when we allow the sanctification process to take place, little by little, we and those around us, begin to see the changes in our lives. It doesn't matter what we have been through or what we have done in the

past, what matters is how we allow God to use it for our good and His glory.

Some of the most difficult times in my life shaped me into who I am today. As I began to hear the words "let your mess become your message" I came into agreement with the calling God placed on my life. I chose to overcome adversity and allow myself to be God's vessel to influence others through the message that only I was uniquely qualified to tell. You have a story too. What is your story that only you are uniquely qualified to tell and influence others by?

> *"You are the light of the world. A town built on a hill cannot be hidden. Neither do people light a lamp and put it under a bowl. Instead they put it on its stand, and it gives light to everyone in the house. In the same way, let your light shine before others, that they may see the good deeds and glorify your Father in heaven. Matthew 5:14-16 (NIV)*

Day 37

THE WRATH

It's with some embarrassment that I admit to having had bouts of anger referred to as "The Wrath of Kim." Am I the only one? You know, those times when you've been hurt by someone who lied to you, was disloyal, or broke their promises, and you reacted inappropriately? God shows us mercy in our weakest moments, and we must learn to extend that same mercy to others as part of our healing process.

I began to see people differently and love them where they were through the revelation that we are all broken and sinful people. God began to transform my heart and show me how to extend the same mercy to others that He shows me. However, the difficult part for me was learning not to mistake showing mercy with reconciliation. While it may be appropriate to extend mercy to others, it would be inappropriate to return to something that is not a part of God's plan for your life.

Sometimes we react to people in anger and later feel regret for the way we acted and the things we said. While anger is an emotion that God gave us and one that is ok to feel, we need to learn to respond appropriately in our anger versus reacting in anger to a situation or person. The good news is that if this sounds anything like you, there is hope! I speak from experience that when the healing process begins to take place, it's not as easy for others to get in there and take away your peace. Reacting in anger wasn't due to the circumstances that surrounded me but rather that I allowed them to make their way into my heart and soul.

> *But they flattered him with their mouths; they lied to him with their tongues. Their heart was not steadfast toward him; they were not faithful to his covenant. Yet he, being compassionate, atoned for their iniquity and did not destroy them; he restrained his anger often and did not stir up all his wrath. He remembered that they were but flesh a wind that passes and comes not again. Psalms 78:36-39 (ESV)*

Day 38

RIGHT PLACE, RIGHT TIME

Have you ever asked yourself as you sit in traffic or miss your alarm if maybe you are exactly where you're supposed to be at that moment? God's timing is always perfect. There are many instances we feel unsettled about where we are, but I have come to consider every situation as an opportunity to reflect upon God's hand in *all* circumstances.

For example, on one occasion arriving somewhere at what I measured an unexpected time turned out to be God's faithful way of bringing betrayal to light. Another thing that comes to mind is a testimony I remember hearing when I was a little girl from a lady at church who talked about missing her usual turn while traveling home from work. She circled back but again missed the turn a second time and later heard about a crime that took place on that street during the time she would have been passing through. Even the stories from 9/11 survivors giving an account of why they were late that fatal day come to my attention.

I'll also never forget the Saturday my dad called to let me know he would be preaching the Sunday morning service if I'd like to come. I remember thinking that I could never know when the last opportunity to hear him preach would be. Little did I know that Sunday morning would be the last time I would ever see my mom alive and well. As I reflected upon the circumstances that transpired surrounding that day, I was awed by how events unfolded. God planned to take my mom, and He was so gracious to allow me the opportunity to see her and have some very special last moments together with her that morning.

Even in the most difficult situations, I've been able to look back and see God's perfect timing. When unexpected circumstances arise, count it as something divine and find peace in where you are. We are just traveling through these seasons of life, and every day we can look forward and trust that God will lead us to where we are meant to be in each moment.

> *"For I know the plans I have for you," declares the LORD, "plans to prosper you and not to harm you, plans to give you hope and a future."*
> *Jeremiah 29:11 (NIV)*

Day 39

STAND FIRM

I can't count the number of times I decided to walk away from something that was *not* bearing fruit in my life, or felt called to walk toward something that would…but I ultimately ended up changing my position on the matter. Even when my spirit was clearly convicting me, the enemy was sure to swoop in and cause double-mindedness.

The Bible says a double-minded person is unstable in all his ways (James 1:8). I had lost faith in my ability to hear my spirit and had such little trust in myself or God, that my life was completely out of balance. I was allowing other things and people to have greater authority over my life than God.

Do not be double-minded in your decision to walk away from people and situations that are interfering with God's plan for your life or allow doubt to keep you from walking toward God's calling. When doubt begins to creep in, stand firm in your convictions. Take those thoughts captive and make them obey Christ.

When I walked away from an unhealthy relationship, it wasn't because I no longer cared about the person or intended to teach a lesson, but rather, through staying I had learned many of my own lessons. When I walked toward God's calling, it wasn't because I had no doubt that it was the right way but rather, I had experienced the unsettling feeling of not walking by faith.

Standing by our convictions is not always the easiest thing to do – but when we surrender to the guidance of the Spirit we can trust in our discernment and have faith in our decisions. Having faith does not mean we are free from any doubt, "Faith is the evidence of things hoped for, the evidence of things not seen" (Hebrews 11:1).

> *We demolish arguments and every pretension that sets itself up against the knowledge of God, and we take captive every thought to make it obedient to Christ. 2 Corinthians 10:5 (NIV)*

Day 40

LOVE YOURSELF

*I*f you're not loving and caring for yourself or looking out for your best interest, who will? It is not selfish to love yourself first; in fact, it's essential.

Making poor choices has happened to all of us at one time or another and while we can't undo what has been done, we can start today by making better choices for ourselves that ultimately affect those around us. It's important to avoid focusing on the things that have brought us pain and suffering, but we can use them for growth.

I was one who always concerned myself with what everyone else was thinking and feeling. I felt responsible for the feelings of other people and I felt the need to fix them, but in the process, I usually abandoned myself. The opposite was also true in that I held others responsible for my feelings and for fixing them.

How many times did I stand by a person who didn't treat me well because I thought they needed me? How many times did I stay too long because I "needed" them so that I would feel loved or validated? Too many to count. Concerning myself with trying to manage the way other people felt about me was another reason I found it difficult to walk away when someone was not treating me well. How would they feel about me? What would they say? Wasn't it my responsibility as a Christian to stay and help "fix" this?

Are you trying to manage the feelings of those around you? The process of trying to manage the feelings of others sets us up to abandon our own. But, when we allow ourselves to experience our feelings – rather than numb them with relationships, alcohol, food, or drugs and express them in an appropriate, respectful manner, then we are taking responsibility for our own feelings and can allow others to do the same.

This is what emotional honesty is all about. Being emotionally honest with yourself and others is how you can begin to love and take care of yourself first. Yes, it's ok to love yourself first. In fact, God says love your neighbor as you love yourself. When you don't love yourself, you can't truly appreciate how to love anyone else. So, how much do you love yourself?

Jesus replied: "'Love the Lord your God with all

your heart and with all your soul and with all your mind.' This is the first and greatest commandment. And the second is like it: 'Love your neighbor as yourself.' Matthew 22: 37-39 (NIV)

Day 41

SEEKING

As I reflected upon past relationships, I realized that I evaluated them based on my craving for attention. I recalled that some were sorely lacking in giving me much attention, and others that provided an unhealthy obsessive level of it. Why did I feed on this attention, but then upon receiving it, push it away only to seek it again?

It wasn't until I started my personal and spiritual growth and recovery journey that I began to understand that I looked to others for what I felt I lacked in myself. I looked to others for love and attention because I couldn't give it to myself. I looked to other people and relationships to be there for me because I didn't know how to be there for myself. I looked to others to develop friendships for me instead of doing the work to grow my own.

In one instance, a person who had a large number of friendships caused me to doubt the consistent dysfunctional level at which I witnessed him operate, because after all, here was this great group of close, supportive friends beside him. The fact is, although people around us may see wonderful qualities we outwardly display, only God truly knows the condition of our heart.

Don't concern yourself with what others around you think or say because at the end of the day God knows who we are. I had a friend speak these words to me that I carried with me through my journey to healing: "Who on God's green earth was this person and their circle of friends that I should care about, in the big scheme of things, what any of them thought of me?"

God will be faithful to remind you that you are who He says you are. When we stop wrestling with God to do things our way and seek Him first, He is faithful to send along everything we truly need. Upon surrendering your way to God's way, you will likely have moments you still desire to fight for what you think is the best way. Resist this temptation and ask yourself why? Are you willing to surrender to God and allow Him to fill in the gaps you feel are lacking?

> *Seek the Kingdom of God above all else, and he will give you everything you need. Luke 12:31 (NLT)*

Day 42

RENOVATIONS UNDERWAY

At one point we have all probably either taken on a renovation project or at least seen a renovation in progress. If you've done one, you know that the very first step is to have a vision and plan. However, some of us have got into the project and realized how unprepared we were for the work ahead. We may not have allocated the time necessary to complete the project, accounted for setbacks or other unexpected things that may have arisen.

A complete restoration involves critical work that's done in hidden spaces such as behind the walls or under the floors and this part can get messy and ugly. Not only must you secure the necessary materials to get the job done, but in most cases, hiring a contractor for a piece of the project is essential. However, when the floor and walls start coming together and the final details such as painting, and decorating begin, you can see the beauty you had originally envisioned.

When something is renovated, the damaged, broken, or outdated structure is improved to a beautiful, new state of being. But as the renovations are underway, you can expect the process to get ugly as you uncover what's underneath; and, you have to be willing to let go of the old to realize and seize the new.

I relate this to my personal growth and recovery journey. I went into the process with a vision, but I was so unprepared for what would be revealed beneath the surface and what was to come. I knew pieces of me were "broken" from my past relationships and I wanted to be restored.

I remember trying to hurry the process along to completion and encountering things that seemed like setbacks. I thought I had implemented all the "materials" I would need by way of reading so many self-help books I couldn't keep count and I set aside time for crushing my personal goals. Yet something was missing.

This is when the "renovation" process truly began. This is when God began to reveal that the broken and damaged pieces of my heart and soul had been there longer than I knew and for reasons other than I was aware. This is when I understood that I couldn't do it. That's right, I said I couldn't do it. I had to do something different and surrender the process to God and allow him to begin the true renovations.

It is often quite difficult to see how we could ever be restored from our broken state. It may be difficult to imagine something good evolving from the looks of things now. I was so thankful that in a very unique way, God gave me an experienced "contractor" aka my personal growth and recovery coach who knew how to guide me through the process and ensure that I began placing the proper coverages in place, for the new me that was emerging!

Something beautiful was emerging beneath the old surface and there was no hiding it! It was apparent every time I tried to put something old back in – it just no longer fit there. I had been restored!

Like renovating any other structure, renovations of the heart and soul take time and the underlying ugly parts are going to be exposed. But that's what brings about something new that God can use for his glory. Renovations would one day be complete but maintaining the new structure, a daily process. I had to learn that I couldn't very well put old things back into the new structure and expect it to remain in its improved state. Something beautiful was emerging beneath the old surface and there was no hiding it! It was apparent every time I tried to put something old back in – it just no longer fit there. I had been restored!

And the one sitting on the throne said, "Look, I am making everything new!" And then he said to me, "Write this down, for what I tell you is trustworthy and true." Revelations 21: 5 (NLT)

Day 43

HEALING THROUGH TEARS

Sometimes we try to hide from our feelings and emotions, but this stunts the process of healing and growth. When we courageously face what we are going through, we can trust that God will bring healing through our tears.

Trusting God in the process of suffering is oftentimes difficult, but the Bible tells us that He is our shelter and hiding place from the storm (Isaiah 4:6). Therefore, we can trust that He is there with us through every difficult moment we are faced with.

I have a "war room" of sorts where I spend time in prayer. I began this when I ended an unhealthy relationship that God was calling me to surrender. This is literally where God healed me, on my knees, in tears, crying out to Him in prayer. These may be the simplest words, but they hold so much truth: "When your pain brings you to your knees you can be healed there."

God has great things planned for you that cannot be fulfilled without letting go of the things that are holding you back and delaying your growth. Not everybody can journey with you to the place God is taking you and it may be a painful process to let go. But just like when David sobbed all night and God was there listening to his every plea, He is here with you now. Change happens when we are on our knees and our spirit is realigned for God's greater purpose.

> *I waited patiently for the Lord to help me, and he turned to me and heard my cry. He lifted me out of the pit of despair, out of the mud and the mire. He set my feet on solid ground and steadied me as I walked along. He has given me a new song to sing, a hymn of praise to our God. Many will see what he has done and be amazed. They will put their trust in the Lord. Psalms 40:1-3 (NLT)*

Day 44

SWORD OF THE SPIRIT

Do you ever read scriptures but forget for a moment that they are written to be applied to your life in the here and now? The Bible is our sword! 2 Timothy 3:16 says that "All Scripture is inspired by God and is useful to teach us what is true and to make us realize what is wrong in our lives. It corrects us when we are wrong and teaches us to do what is right."

God speaks in many ways, but most profound to me is when I come across a scripture that I may have read multiple times, yet during one particular season of life I'm reading those same exact words as if I'd never seen them before – they just seem to come to life!

I remember coming across a verse like this and it spoke to me. It is used in the context of growing spiritually in all of God's ways. When I placed my name in it, my whole mindset changed.

"[Kim] is like a tree planted by streams of water, which yields its fruit in season and whose leaf does not wither. Whatever [she] does prospers" (Psalms 1:3).

Let this be a reminder of just how powerful God's word is. When you feel like you're struggling to hear God's voice, open His Word, add your name to the scriptures, personalize them, and see them come to life in you!

> *For the word of God is alive and powerful. It is sharper than the sharpest two-edged sword, cutting between soul and spirit, between joint and marrow. It exposes our innermost thoughts and desires. Hebrews 4:12 (NLT)*

Day 45

ENCOURAGEMENT

At the time of this writing, I am celebrating another birthday. Another year has come and gone. While not a whole lot changed outwardly, on the inside God continues to change me into someone I almost don't recognize.

I'm so thankful for the birthday gifts I received, but the gifts I will forever be most grateful for are those that led me into the journey of personal and spiritual growth and recovery from emotional trauma. I will forever be a huge advocate of this and I'm looking forward to God unfolding the vision He has for the next chapter of my life. I'm so thankful for every single person that God placed in my path that brought me to this point. The good, the bad, the joy, and the pain – all of it has become a gift that God has given purpose to.

The Bible tells us that Isaac planted in a drought but reaped a hundredfold (Genesis 26). When I planted my first seed in the direction in which God was leading me, I would have considered myself in a season of drought. I didn't even realize I was planting a seed.

While I hoped what I was doing would encourage someone, it was truly a way of holding myself accountable. I couldn't imagine inspiring anyone else, but I trusted in the One who could use all of these things for my good and I began taking the next right step each day. God began using my honesty and vulnerability to inspire hope and encouragement in those around me.

God placed a desire in my heart to plant seeds of inspiration all around me through my story. Wherever you may be on your journey through life, be encouraged and know that God can do amazing things when you show up and do your part. I certainly wouldn't say I have it all perfectly together, but that's the beauty of it. You can start where you are, and God will meet you there.

I love this verse in Philippians 3:12-14 from The Message Bible where Paul writes, "I'm not saying that I have this all together, that I have it made. But I am well on my way, reaching out for Christ, who has so wondrously reached out for me. Friends don't get me wrong: By no means do I count myself an expert in all of this, but I've got my eye on the goal, where God is beckoning us onward – to Jesus. I'm off and running, and I'm not turning back."

> *So let's not get tired of doing what is good. At just the right time we will reap a harvest of blessing if we don't give up." Galatians 6:9 (NLT)*

Day 46

SHIFTING YOUR PERSPECTIVE

As parents, when you're at home and your young children are there but they're quiet, you can bet they are up to something! As Christians, we know that God is always there. Yet sometimes we are in a place where we just can't seem to hear Him, but you can be sure He is up to something.

We hear it said all of the time, "Let Go and Let God." Of course, we can't let go of everything...we have responsibilities to maintain, but we can learn to let go of those things we can't control. Yes, God is in control of everything, but He won't control what you choose to prioritize in your life. God doesn't want to control us; He gives us free will to choose. But He *does* want us to be transformed and sometimes that happens in some very uncomfortable ways.

When we go through seasons that cause us to start asking questions like, "How long is this going to last?", or "When will things be different?" – we have to stop and shift our perspective to consider why we might be in this uncomfortable place and how we are being transformed through it. Sometimes we will find ourselves in a painful situation because we chose to go ahead without God. Other times it could be something like a pandemic that causes us to start asking these questions. But the one certainty we all have is that amid every situation, God is there.

I've come to understand that in every circumstance there is a lesson that can be learned and an opportunity to shift my perspective and allow it to transform me. No matter how quiet God may seem at any given time as you draw close to him you will find He has been there working behind the scenes all along. So, consider asking yourself the right questions like, "What have I learned through this?" and start bringing positivity into every situation because you can always trust that God is up to something good.

> *But do not overlook this one fact, beloved, that with the Lord one day is a thousand years, and a thousand years as one day. The Lord is not slow to fulfill his promise as some count slowness, but is patient toward you, not wishing that any should perish, but that all should reach repentance. 2 Peter 3: 8-9 (ESV)*

Day 47

CHILDHOOD BREAKTHROUGHS

Our childhood contributes to how we relate to people as adults and as I began to pray for the Holy Spirit to reveal these characteristics in me, I was given some awe-inspiring breakthroughs.

When I first began my personal growth and recovery journey and was asked to look at my childhood as a clue to how I relate to people today, I couldn't find the connection. I saw my childhood as a normal, loving childhood. I couldn't understand how my approval-seeking and validation-needing behavior or my need to control and fix things could have anything to do with my seemingly normal upbringing.

As I began inviting the Holy Spirit in to reveal these things, God showed up in a powerful way and gave me clarity on some root issues. I understood that as innocently and unintentionally as it was, my childhood contributed to some of my unhealthy ways of relating to people. In Daniel 2:47 (ESV) it says, "The king answered and said to Daniel, 'Truly, your God is God of gods and Lord of kings, and a revealer of mysteries, for you have been able to reveal this mystery.'" I began to celebrate the breakthroughs as they were revealed, and the healing began.

God speaks in different ways, but I hear him most when I pray and then open His Word to scriptures that seem to just jump off the page with insight on the very thing I'm praying for or going through. It's always an Ah-ha moment and it's an incredible experience that confirms He is there with me. However, there have been times when I prayed and didn't seem to get the answer I was looking for. I now understand that these moments were no different. God was faithful in those moments. He was there, He saw what I was going through, and He was careful to only reveal what I could bear to understand at that moment.

God says, "There is so much more I want to tell you, but you can't bear it now" (John 16:12). Invite the Holy Spirit to reveal those things in you that need healing, continue to pray, and trust God in His timing.

Then he said to me, "Fear not, Daniel, for from the first day that you set your heart to understand and humbled yourself before your God, your words have been heard, and I have come because of your words. Daniel 10:12 (ESV)

Day 48

VALIDATION AND APPROVAL-SEEKING

Often unintentional on the part of a caregiver, children who feel as though they have a standard to meet but always fall short of, begin to seek approval out of a limiting belief that they can't do anything good enough. Sometimes children hear a message that says, "You aren't good enough and you can't do anything right, but I love you." Not feeling good enough but still being loved and needed can leave a child feeling invalidated.

As an adult, if you find that you're allowing yourself to behave in ways that are contrary to your beliefs and who God has called you to be, it may be time to address your validation and approval-seeking needs. I tried to find my worth in exterior things. In relationships, I looked for validation and approval to correct my feelings of inadequacy. When I was complimented and felt needed,

I stayed – even through the repeated, unhealthy behaviors of my partner.

As I began to understand my own behaviors and their root issues, I asked God to remove the character defects in me that left me seeking this approval and validation from others. I began to surrender the pattern of unhealthy relationships that seemed to be forming and chose to begin a journey of personal growth and recovery.

Through this healing process, my need for validation and approval from others began to fade. My relationship with Christ changed and I understood the love He has for me. We are God's children, created in His image. He is the only one that went to the cross to die for you. There is no greater validation than that.

I praise you, for I am fearfully and wonderfully made. Wonderful are your works; my soul knows it very well. Psalms 139:14 (ESV)

Day 49

FIXING

As a child, knowing that you are loved and needed, but feeling that you aren't good enough, can lead to many unhealthy behaviors. Children may begin to believe that all the wrong things that happen must be their fault if they are needed yet whatever they do isn't good enough. This often brings about a struggle with the need to "fix" things.

As adults, these children become people who try to control and fix everything. For me, even when things weren't "broken" I saw them that way. On the rare occasion that all appeared well, it was like it was so unfamiliar to me, that it seemed I was sure to break it again just to "fix it." This became a pattern I recognized in my relationships.

Sometimes we are drawn to people who are overly dependent on us, believing that they need us in their life. We allow them to treat us poorly and sometimes abusively. We are drawn to familiarity and this sometimes causes us to stay in broken relationships to "fix" everything because of our desire to be needed and validated.

It is not our job to fix anyone. It is our job only to love others. If you are seeking approval and validation from others, take those needs to the Lord. Through this process, you find your worth is not in other people's approval or validation of you. You are worthy of respect and you deserve to be treated well and loved unconditionally.

> *"A new commandment I give to you, Love one another. As I have loved you, so you must love one another. By this everyone will know that you are my disciples, if you love one another."*
> *John 13:34-35 (NIV)*

Day 50

PATIENCE

We practice patience in gardening from the time we plant the first seed, to the time we see the harvest. This same patience is necessary for your spiritual growth and healing journey.

When we plant a seed, we trust that it will grow even though we see no evidence at that moment. We know that the time from seed to harvest depends on many factors, but we rarely doubt that the harvest will come. We know there is nothing we can do to rush the process; we simply trust the process. We understand that it takes time for something beautiful to grow.

Why then, is it so difficult to trust the process of our own growth and healing? We surrender what we feel God has asked us to, we begin the work that we are called to do, and then we get frustrated or doubtful when we don't see the immediate fruits of our labor.

We begin to lose patience and question if we heard God correctly. But immediate results are never the way any process works.

In the same way, we trust the gardening process, we can and must have faith that God will see his plan for our lives to completion. Don't doubt that your healing is coming. We must have patience with ourselves even through affliction and be persistent in prayer.

Rejoice in hope; be patient in affliction; be persistent in prayer. Romans 12:12 (HCSB)

Day 51

DISAPPOINTMENT

In a romantic relationship, I sometimes found happiness only when I sensed a "fantasy hero." One who saved me from what I thought I was lacking and provided what I thought I needed. This was a recipe for disappointment because every person has their flaws. However, when I repeatedly received the message, "I'm sorry, it'll be different next time" in a relationship beginning as a very young adult, I reached a point when I tried to become emotionally distant. I no longer desired to "need" or expect anything so that I wouldn't be disappointed.

Trying to deny myself from having an emotional connection caused a lot of resentment and anger. I felt as though I carried everything in my relationship and although I sometimes reached the point of anger that caused me to speak up for what I needed, unfortunately in an unhealthy way, it was a fearful experience to think

I wasn't going to get it. And once again, not getting what I needed would leave me feeling unworthy.

It was apparently just as fearful when on occasion, I got what I thought I needed from people – because then, it was *so unfamiliar* to me that I had no idea how to react or deal with it. An example of this was seen in my inability to accept a compliment. For most of my life when I was complimented, I could not simply accept it or say thank you; instead, I would point out the reasons I saw things as a disappointment or not good enough.

The negative messages that are trapped in your mind that scream things like you are not good enough, or don't expect your needs to be met, must be replaced with God's truth. God's truth is that He will provide for you and meet your every need. You are so worthy that He sent His only Son to die for you. When you allow God to satisfy your needs, it is then that relationships with others can prosper.

Since he did not spare even his own Son but gave him up for us all, won't he also give us everything else?
Romans 8:32 NLT

Day 52

CHILDHOOD LOSSES

Understanding what makes us function the way we do as adults starts with some digging into our childhood. For example, losses suffered in childhood can contribute to feelings of abandonment in adulthood.

During my childhood, I moved several times. In the process of moving from Ohio to Florida and from one city there to another, back to Ohio, and then to Texas, I felt the loss of some very close friends and family as well as church and school connections. In addition, I suffered a couple of major illnesses. I had severe asthma as a child and remember many times literally gasping for air, unable to breathe as I looked to my mom to administer my rescue inhaler.

In second grade as I started to leave my classroom, I found myself unable to walk. The next thing I remember is being in the hospital with a diagnosis of junior rheumatoid arthritis in my knee. I believe my hospital stay was a week or two. As traumatic as a loss of breath from asthma was to experience, my mom leaving me at the hospital one day seemed to be *more* than I could manage. I can't remember the situation. I believe she was going home to get some of my things, but the memory I have is fear. I remember following her in a wheelchair, crying, and in my mind questioning if she was upset with me and if she was coming back.

I don't know why these memories are embedded in my mind but as an adult, they contributed to my fear of abandonment in relationships as well as my efforts to keep anyone from getting upset with me. Somewhere in childhood between frequently moving, and experiencing illness, I lost my sense of security, and the idea that I would always need someone to take care of me was born.

I walked away from these traumatic experiences believing that my well-being and survival depended on *others*. As painful as some memories can be, I thank God for revealing them to me so they could be addressed.

> Somewhere in childhood between frequently moving, and experiencing illness, I lost my sense of security, and the idea that I would always need someone to take care of me was born.

If you suffered losses in childhood, you may carry around fears that you aren't even aware of. I encourage you to ask God to reveal these things to you, so they can be healed. The truth is, whatever we need – whether it be our next breath or to be cared for by someone, God will provide. When we put our trust in Him, fear begins to dissipate.

Look at the birds of the air; they neither sow nor reap nor gather into barns, and yet your heavenly Father feeds them. Are you not of more value than they? And which of you by being anxious can add a single hour to his span of life? Matthew 6:26-27 (ESV)

Day 53

ANXIETY

nxiety and panic once played a big part in my life. Fear and anxiety controlled most of the choices I made. This motivated me to stay in toxic situations and kept me from using the talents God gave me. I had little vision for my future, all I could see was uncertainty. But as I began to practice *surrendering* things that were out of my control, anxiety lost its grip on me.

In the past, I tried to take control of *every* situation. This ultimately led to greater feelings of anxiety when things didn't play out the way I wanted them to. I tried to control other people, how much they drank, how often they chose to go to church, how they spent their money, how they took care of their children, and basically how to live their entire life as if I was the expert.

I made it my job to convict anyone who didn't have the same sense of right and wrong that I did. Looking back, it was exhausting not only for me but those closest to me. I can see why anxiety played such a big part in my life. I remember calling my dad many times asking him to pray with me because I was in the midst of a panic attack as a result of anxiety. The first thing he would say is "Don't worry about anything. Pray about everything. Thank God for what he has already done and for what he's about to do."

We can never be certain what the days ahead hold but we can be certain that God is in control even when we don't like what's happening around us. Nothing happens that is not a part of His sovereign will. God has given us free will to choose even when our choices bring about pain and suffering. Today, I can be thankful for my struggle with anxiety because it has made me who I am and it's another opportunity to share where I've been and what God has brought me through.

> *Don't worry about anything; instead, pray about everything. Tell God what you need, and thank him for all he has done. Then you will experience God's peace, which exceeds anything we can understand. His peace will guard your hearts and minds as you live in Christ Jesus. Philippians 4: 6-7 (NLT)*

Day 54

PERSONAL BOUNDARIES

Consider a fence gate that is sometimes locked to protect a homeowner from intruders. In this same way establishing healthy personal boundaries is key to protecting ourselves.

I like to use this familiar analogy of a fence around a home in relation to personal boundaries because the fence is used to signify the property line between our home and our neighbors, and each has a gate that allows us and our friends to come and go. When we use the gate, it should always be with the intention of everyone returning to their own space.

But when we don't have healthy boundaries in place, we can become enmeshed in someone else's space. In other words, we get all tangled up in someone else, we lose our sense of self and begin to mirror their wants and needs. At that point, we have failed to stand in our individuality and protect our standard of integrity which leads to feelings of resentment. Then we begin to blame the other party for *our* lack of having healthy boundaries in place.

It's our responsibility to set healthy boundaries in our relationships that can protect us from unnecessary harm. Some of us allow people to walk through our gate who haven't earned our trust. We allow them access to our entire "property" but wonder why we suffer so much loss. The bible tells us to love, give, and sacrifice but it doesn't tell us to abandon ourselves and our emotional health or stand for disrespect of our morals and values.

Prior to doing my own self-growth work, the concept of boundaries was all very foreign to me. I've learned to keep the gate closed to those people who have not earned my trust and to lock it when someone has betrayed my trust and shows no sign of true change. It doesn't mean that I'm upset, or that I don't care about the person; instead, it means that I love myself and the other person enough to be honest about what I will and will not accept.

The most essential boundary I have in place is a zero-tolerance for lies and deception. The bible tells us, "No one who practices deceit will dwell in my house; no one who speaks falsely will stand in my presence" (Psalms 101:7).

In maintaining a healthy relationship, each person must clearly identify their personal boundaries and while it may be appropriate to share our space for a while, we each return to our own side of the fence.

We do not invade anyone else's space, nor do we allow anyone to invade ours. We set limits on what is acceptable behavior and while many things in a relationship can be negotiated, we don't negotiate our morals and values. We learn to say no when it's appropriate and we do not allow ourselves to be manipulated or controlled by anyone else. We give ourselves the permission to be who we are and know we are worthy of God's best.

> *Christ has set us free to live a free life. So take your stand! Never again let anyone put a harness of slavery on you. Galatians 5:1 (MSG)*

Day 55

CODEPENDENCY

Somewhere in the childhood of a codependent adult, a form of trauma took place that hampered their ability to relate to others in an emotionally mature way.

While there are too many symptoms of codependency to list here, at the core of it all is the inability to relate appropriately to the self. Difficulty in setting boundaries and being true to one's self is often at the top of the list because codependents find their worth from pleasing others and gaining their approval and acceptance. They feel responsible for everyone else's problems and for fixing them, so they insert themselves into the middle of other people's lives and give their opinion on how one should think, feel, and act – mistakenly believing they know what is best for everyone.

When the idea of codependency was first brought to my attention, I remember saying that *none* of the symptoms that were presented were me. However, there are so many ways the symptoms manifest themselves in people and I discovered all of the above in myself.

Before I began my personal development and recovery work, I found myself in an unhealthy relationship and my emotional health was deeply entangled and dependent on it. I felt the need to fix things immediately, out of fear of losing someone or their approval of me. At one point I began to neglect family and friends and was all-consumed by this intimate relationship.

Regretfully, I ignored my morals and values to gain the approval of others. I found it abnormally difficult to separate myself when I was not being treated well – partly because I looked for my identity in the approval and acceptance of others.

In healthy relationships, we should be able to depend on each other for support, but in codependency, it goes far beyond this in a very unhealthy way. Have you ever found yourself looking for your worth in being needed by another person or losing your individuality to their interests? Do you find yourself inserting your opinion in nearly every situation? Do you think you know what's best for others or do you try to fix their thinking? Do you find others getting upset with you when you're "just trying to help"? You may not recognize these things within yourself, but you can ask God to reveal them to you and find healing.

Blessed is the one who perseveres under trial because, having stood the test, that person will receive the crown of life that the Lord has promised to those who love him. James 1:12 (NIV)

Day 56

EMOTIONAL HONESTY

*E*motional honesty involves being in tune with your feelings and being able to express them in a healthy way. While honesty and communication should be at the core of every relationship, we often censor our emotions to please others and abandon our own feelings.

I loved others so much, or what I thought was loving them, that I didn't feel comfortable being honest about who I was, what I was feeling, or what I needed. So instead, I tried manipulating the thoughts, feelings, and actions of others to get what I needed.

Although my radar for detecting and rejecting even the slightest bit of anyone else's attempt to control me was off-the-charts, I didn't detect it when I would attempt to control others. When these attempts at controlling others to feel and act in the manner I needed failed, my whole world seemed to come crashing down.

My feelings and my obsessive thoughts were out of control, but I tried hiding my imperfections from everyone and maintained a façade of perfectionism and having it all together.

When I first began to test the tool of emotional honesty, it back-fired many times. I couldn't understand why using this new tool of expressing my feelings in a respectful way didn't always work out for good. What I learned was that some people are just not in a place to hear your truth without feeling offended by it. Other times we may find that we still had some hidden lingering traces of trying to control the outcome of expressing our feelings. Using this tool effectively requires detaching from any expectations.

It is such a relief when we are able to respectfully express what we are feeling, and let others manage their own feelings. It is a long and difficult process for some to learn to use this tool effectively, but if we remain diligent in working on using it, we can see our relationships begin to prosper. When you have weak moments, and you don't get things right, trust that through your weakness you will become stronger.

> *For the sake of Christ, then, I am content with weakness, insults, hardships, persecutions, and calamities. For when I am weak, then I am strong. 2 Corinthians 12:10 (ESV)*

Day 57

CONFIDENCE

God has gone before you, stands beside you, and walks behind you. Whatever situation you're in, be confident you are not alone. Each time I have ever gone to a job interview I expected to walk away with the job, and I can only remember once, as a very young adult, that I didn't. I'm sure many things factored into my success such as being prepared, having a good resume, matching qualifications, looking my best, and such. But I believed I was the best person for the job, and I was prepared to portray that and back it up with my experience and qualifications.

Yet somehow, I just couldn't find this confidence when God called me to carry out His work. I wasn't sure how I qualified for that job. I didn't feel prepared and things from my "resume" didn't look the best. But what I find is that every time I listen and step out in faith He shows up and gives me the tools I need to complete the assignment.

You see, God doesn't call the qualified, He qualifies the called. He takes our mess and turns it into a message that only we are uniquely qualified to tell. So, that thing you've been struggling to overcome does not disqualify you. What disqualifies you are the negative thoughts of yourself or those of others about you, that you absorb as truth. God didn't give anybody else what He gave you, He didn't show them what He has shown you. So when others can't see what you see, or see where you're going that's ok, it may just be that they're unable yet to go there with you.

Prior to the start of sharing my journey publicly, my mentor told me that we don't need to have overcome something entirely before we can start sharing our journey through it.

When we accept that we won't receive support from everyone we think we should, and we lay our expectations down, it is then that we can gain confidence knowing that the only approval we need is God's. He is the only one who decides if you're qualified for His work. So, be confident that you're hired!

> *The Lord himself goes before you and will be with you; he will never leave you nor forsake you. Do not be afraid; do not be discouraged.*
> *Deuteronomy 31:8 (NIV)*

Day 58

POWER OF WORDS

*D*id your parents ever tell you that if you can't say anything nice, don't say anything at all? There was some true wisdom in those words. Never underestimate the power of your spoken words.

It's a continuous work in progress for many of us to learn to either say something positive or say nothing at all. Sometimes we say the wrong things to someone else, and other times we are our own worst enemy speaking discouraging words over ourselves. But when you understand how powerful your spoken words are, you'll begin to think twice about what comes out of your mouth.

I once heard that when you learn to control your tongue, you start to gain power over your life. Unfortunately, I didn't learn this lesson until later in life. The bible talks about the tongue being able to pierce and I admit I struggled to get it under control. When someone hurt me, I could cut them with my tongue. What I've learned is that the control I have over my tongue reflects where I am spiritually in that moment. I also learned that it's so much more uncomfortable to make amends for my words and actions than it is to hold my tongue until I've prayed about the situation and I can respond in a respectful and emotionally honest way.

As critical as I could be of others, I was most critical of myself. But through my personal and spiritual growth and recovery journey, I began to speak truth into every situation based upon what God's word says. When someone hurt me and I struggled to forgive them, I spoke words of forgiveness, and my feelings followed because we've *all* sinned and fallen short.

When I felt I was too weak to walk away from a toxic relationship, I spoke words of truth and continued to take the next right step because God is my strength and my refuge. And, even in my struggle to find my worth and identity in Christ, I spoke it anyway, and my belief followed. Consider this, God created the heavens and the earth by ***speaking*** them into existence.

Remember, while God knows our every thought, the enemy doesn't. However, once you speak those negative thoughts into existence, the enemy will be waiting to use your own words to torment you. So, while we can't control negative thoughts from entering our mind, don't dare speak them out of your mouth; instead, the bible tells us to take every thought captive and make it obedient to Christ. Remember that the bible is sharper than any two-edged sword, so speak it and the enemy will flee. When you can't say anything nice, don't settle for saying nothing at all, speak life over yourself and over every situation because the bible says the power of life and death are in the tongue.

Let no corrupting talk come out of your mouths,
but only such is good for building up, as fits the
occasion, that it may give grace to those that hear.
Ephesians 4:29 (ESV)

Day 59

TRUSTING AGAIN

Trust is the foundation of any relationship. Without it, the relationship can't survive in a healthy way because while many differences can be overcome, when there is no mutual trust, there is nothing to build upon. There will always be risks involved in trusting someone, so how do you know when it is safe? Your priority must be to put God above anyone else in your life. When you allow anything or anyone in your life to have greater authority than God, you'll be missing the peace that only He can bring.

God works in amazing ways. He can bring healing to unresolved issues from your past that hamper your ability to recognize trustworthy characteristics. We are all sinful by nature, so at some point, we will be hurt by another person. However, what I've learned is to recognize the difference between being *hurt* and being *harmed*. Subjecting yourself to the same repeated unhealthy behaviors causes emotional *harm*. I allowed myself to be repeatedly exposed to so much harmful behavior that I developed a very high tolerance for it. Without even realizing, I became somewhat numb to it.

Emotional pain has a way of causing us to withdraw, and contrary to popular belief, time does *not* heal all. Not unlike a physical injury that sometimes requires physical therapy, I needed healing that came through the work in recovery and spiritual growth. This not only led to healing, but I gained the tools to better assess the characteristics of a trustworthy person and to trust my discernment.

So, while you can't fully protect yourself from the risks involved in the decision to trust, without taking the risk you'll never see the reward. Remember, trusting someone is a decision you choose to make so ask God to lead you in the process.

> *Behold, I am sending you out as sheep in the midst of wolves, so be wise as serpents and innocent as doves. Matthew 10:16 (ESV)*

Day 60

RECOGNIZING CHANGE

Have you ever wanted someone's values to align with yours so you tried desperately to see a change in who they really were to fit the potential of who you thought they could be?

I remember showing up at the park one day at the start of the summer wearing my hat and sunglasses. I did this a lot on the weekends during the summer months. But on this day for some reason, it seemed that I had never done it before. I saw my grandson playing and said, "Hi! Are you having fun?" His response was, "Do I know you?" Apparently, not even my daughters recognized me at first. I thought it was strange that my own family didn't recognize me. Unfortunately, while recognizing change from the outside is obvious, changes occurring within are not so apparent. Understanding how to recognize when a true change has occurred is an important step to take prior to making an effort to rebuild a broken relationship.

When someone betrays your trust, it can be one of the most difficult things to rebuild. Not only do you begin to question if this person is who they say they are, but it's also difficult not to analyze every situation through that lens of betrayal.

Although as a Christian I knew conviction of the heart was the job of the Holy Spirit, I repeatedly made the mistake of trying to convict someone of their wrongdoing. I had to face the fact that when someone is not convicted on their own, that's a sign of the condition of their heart and where they are spiritually. While it may sometimes be appropriate to rebuild a relationship, it's not without first recognizing when a true change has occurred.

A repentant heart or trustworthy person will not make excuses, rationalize, blame, or justify their inappropriate behavior. Words like, "I said I'm sorry" or "that's in the past" are *not* signs of a remorseful heart. A sincerely repentant or trustworthy person cares how their actions affected you and they'll be willing to address the situation until you feel comfortable letting it go.

Trust yourself enough not to doubt your God-given discernment. I was great at ignoring mine and distorting reality. The reality concerning some relationships you keep trying to build upon is that the only thing motivating change is you. There is no self-motivation for change and certainly no signs of a truly contrite heart on the part of the other person.

Character flaws like lying, deception, and such are deeply embedded in a person and didn't develop overnight. Without a true desire to have a relationship with Christ and to do the hard work that results in real change, the best predictor of the future is the past.

> *The mind governed by the flesh is death, but the*
> *mind governed by the Spirit is life and peace.*
> *Romans 8:6 (NIV)*

Day 61

HIDDEN WOUNDS

About 15 years ago I began to feel a lot of pain in my stomach. I have a very high tolerance for pain, so I ignored the symptoms and didn't see a doctor until I was literally bent over unable to stand up. By this time, emergency surgery was required. I had an incarcerated hernia that became strangulated, which cut off the blood flow to the intestines and abdominal tissues.

When I woke up, I was told that due to an infection hidden beneath the surface, the surgeon left a 4" incision from my navel down, open to heal from the inside out. Every day after, until completely healed, I had to place a rag in my mouth to bite down on, as the bandage was ripped out of this open wound and replaced with a new one. It was the most excruciating physical pain I've ever felt in my life.

I tell you this to relate the experience to the process we often underestimate in recovering from emotional wounds. We can develop a very high tolerance for emotional pain. When we ignore the symptoms it often leads to more pain and even feelings of being cut off from our spiritual source of life. I left a 27-year marriage with an open wound that was never healed, and then entered another relationship that added severe injury to the already-open wound. When it became so painful that I could no longer stand it, I knew I had to let God operate, so I surrendered to another type of "surgery."

It's a special story in itself of how God placed a recovery coach in my path at that perfect time. As I walked through the process of healing, every step felt like that bandage was being ripped off again – and the pain was almost unbearable. But I was being healed from the inside out. I repeatedly had to ask God to make me willing to let go of things that were not His best for me because I *still* wanted what I wanted. It's a whole other story to tell you the ways that God has been faithful in doing that.

> I repeatedly had to ask God to make me willing to let go of things that were not His best for me because I still wanted what I wanted.

When our wounds heal, they leave scars. In the summer when I wear a bikini, I often wrap a sarong around my waist to hide the physical scars from my surgery. But I do my best to accept it as a beautiful part of me that was once wounded and now healed. In this same way, I'm learning to embrace the scars that are not visible to others but remain on my heart, as a beautiful reminder of the pain that I endured and now look to God to protect me and guide me away from.

We often neglect the fact that we are not merely physical bodies. We are made up of the spirit, soul, and body. In the same way that we don't ignore our physical injuries, our emotional injuries require attention as well – and God is the Healer of deep emotional wounds.

Psalms 147:3 He heals the brokenhearted and binds up their wounds. Psalms 147:3 (NIV)

Day 62

FIGHTING BATTLES

*S*urrendering your unhealthy ways is like fighting a battle…and the way to overcome your enemy is to move forward. Battles are won by standing firm or moving forward in the right direction with dedication and focus. If you retreat, you not only *delay* your victory but you risk being overcome by the enemy.

Every time you turn back, you risk suffering more wounds and loss. When the enemy tries to torment you with doubt and fear, when he tells you lies that you can't win this battle, and he tries to deceive you into running back to the comfort of familiar misery, look to the One who has already won the victory and utterly defeated the enemy.

As I went through the process of surrendering my will to God's will, I had to ask Him to reveal what was broken in me that kept me turning back to those ways that were harmful. As He began revealing the wounds in me that needed healing, I had to get on my knees and begin allowing God to fight the battle that was raging inside of me.

I cried out to Him, told Him every feeling of sadness, anger, guilt, hurt, and everything else I had. Then I held my hands up and said, "Here God, you take it." I surrendered. I laid it at His feet and left it there as I began moving forward in the right direction. I remembered that this battle I was fighting wasn't against flesh and blood enemies – it wasn't against other human beings, but rather against the dark world.

Let God's loving arms be the arms you fall into. Allow Him to comfort you and bring you peace. Every time the enemy tries to torment your mind and every time you want to fall back into the trap of those unhealthy ways, remember the devil is a liar! God will give you strength each day to get to the next. God's grace is new *every* morning. You *will* get through this, one day at a time. It's time to surrender that familiar place you've been living in for so long – and move forward to victory.

> *You will not need to fight in this battle. Stand firm, hold your position, and see the salvation of the Lord on your behalf, O Judah and Jerusalem.' Do not be afraid and do not be dismayed. Tomorrow go out against them, and the Lord will be with you."*
> *2 Chronicles 20:17 (ESV)*

Day 63

FOCUS ON THE FUTURE

What we focus on is magnified. Therefore, as we focus on the vision for our future rather than the failures of our past, where we are going becomes greater than what we are going through.

Sometimes we are so focused on past disappointments that we fail to even have a vision for our future. We beat ourselves up over things we have done wrong and often replay in our head *all* the bad things that have been done to us. I can't tell you how many times I've replayed a story in my head and wondered how things could have been different if I had done this or that.

We analyze past situations as if we could put a different ending on what has already happened. As I continued to focus on the wrong that had been done to me or what I had done wrong to someone else, I was unable to see past that point in time. We can't change the past, but we *can* change our future! We not only have to let go of those things in the past but we must also let go of any worry we have about the future. We do not have to worry about the future ahead of us, we have to be led by God toward it.

Although it's important to recognize the wrong you have done to others and learn from those that have been done to you, it's equally important not to dwell there. Make amends when appropriate and move forward with a focus on your future. Understand that those who have hurt you are broken and are hurt themselves. Surround yourself with positive people and ask the Lord to heal you from your past. Trust that God has already paved the way for your future.

> *"Forget the former things; do not dwell on the past. See, I am doing a new thing! Now it springs up; do you not perceive it? I am making a way in the wilderness and streams in the wasteland.*
> *Isaiah 43: 18-19 (NIV)*

Day 64

LOVE

I once heard a message in which the diversity of the word "love" was discussed. For example, we say things like "I love this movie" as well as "I love you, mom." These are obviously two different meanings of the word. We wouldn't say we love our mom the same way we love a movie.

Love is a word that is often used out of context. There is a beautiful verse in 1 Corinthians that talks about what love is. I love this verse (no pun intended there) so much that it is framed in my home.

However, in my decision to leave a toxic relationship, this verse was used against me as he endlessly repeated the words, "Love endures all things." He would chide that if I really loved him, the Bible says love conquers all. I struggled for a while with this, until participating in a 14-day challenge called "Let Love In." Each day I read the verse below and allowed my spirit to guide me into what God wanted me to hear.

What I took away from the daily reading of this verse was profound. I was looking to fill a void within myself by staying in an unhealthy relationship and that was not love. I was constantly pleaded with and guilted into coming back and that was *not* love. I believe we both sought intimacy to fill our deficits and that isn't true love.

True agape love seeks to benefit the other person, and it seeks the highest good of the other person. My love ultimately endured because I chose to let him go when I knew I couldn't love him the way he should be loved nor was he capable of loving me in a healthy way.

It was more harmful to both of us to stay in the relationship. When I handed him over to God and asked God to take care of him and love him the way that only He could, I was showing a true agape love that the Bible talks about. I wasn't returning and leaving the relationship anymore out of my selfish desires and needs. Instead, I wanted the best not only for me but also for him; so, I released him to find a love that I couldn't give him nor could he give me.

> *Love is patient and kind. Love is not jealous or boastful or proud or rude. It does not demand its own way. It is not irritable, and it keeps no record*

*of being wronged. It does not rejoice about
injustice but rejoices whenever the truth wins out.
Love never gives up, never loses faith, is always
hopeful, and endures through every circumstance.
1 Corinthians 13:4-7 (NLT*

Day 65

DO UNTO OTHERS

I once saw a shirt that said, "Hold my halo, I'm about to do unto others as they have done unto me." I thought it was funny, but the sad reality was the shirt once "fit" in the biggest size it came. The actual bible verse is said to be the golden rule, "Do unto others as you would have them do unto you" (Matthew 7:12).

This rule teaches us the ethical principle of morality. It is the empathy we are to show others when someone does us wrong. God's instruction is to handle it according to this "golden rule."

Many times, when we are wronged, we see ourselves with a halo that doesn't belong. We forget that we have also hurt others. When we have been wronged, whether we choose to do unto others as the shirt suggests or follow what the Bible suggests, can be a clear indication and reflection of our relationship with Christ.

My old way of reacting to someone when they hurt me was to lash out in anger. I recently had an experience in which I still considered doing just that. But the fact that I was able to walk away with a gentle spirit was a true testament to the spiritual condition of my heart.

Getting out of your own head and showing compassion towards others in the midst of your suffering is healing. My dad always told me to consider how others treat me as a reflection of what they're going through.

We don't know what someone has been through that led them to the actions that hurt us. But both their behavior and ours will show where we are in relation to our walk with God. So, even during situations that can't be reconciled, we can choose to follow the golden rule and keep our head held high knowing we showed decency to others that we expect for ourselves.

> *So in everything, do to others what you would have them do to you, for this sums up the Law and the Prophets. Matthew 7:12 (NIV)*

Day 66

PUTTING IN TIME

There is this place between the excitement we have for our vision of the future and seeing the results – it's called "putting in the time". During holidays when I tend to eat more than usual, I often say that I have to put in the time for doing the crime, referring to the gym. But true changes that take place in the gym require a commitment to time as well as a knowledgeable strategy. To gain more muscle, you have to challenge your body to do more – so providing the proper nutrition, rest, and resistance training is a key part of this strategy. It is through the process of our muscles reaching the point of failure that growth occurs.

The requirements to see changes on the inside are very much the same as the outside. Our patterns of behavior and interacting with others are deeply ingrained personality traits by the time we are adults. Changing these patterns of behavior is difficult and requires time, commitment, insight into our behaviors, and a strategy to effectively alter them.

Unfortunately, some people never reach the point of failure to see real growth occur. In other words, they only resist to the degree of change, but not to the point of failure. For example, in relationships, a pattern of leaving someone only to find the same issues in another will continue to repeat – unless the person is brought to the point of failure and resists their ingrained patterns of behavior where growth can occur. Similar to the gym, this requires a commitment to consistent resistance training, proper rest, *and* nutrition by way of spiritual food.

My mentor reminded me that there is a place between our exciting vision for the future and the fulfillment of it that calls for us to stay grounded in doing the hard work…even when it's no longer exciting and can be exhausting. How true this is.

In just about everything we do, whether it's getting a degree, or finishing a project, there is a place in the middle that requires dedication to get to the finish line. But can you imagine what you could accomplish by feeding your spirit every few hours or by training heavily in the word of God? How we would grow! It's not easy to follow the strategy that leads to true change and growth, but when we have a relationship with Christ, the desire to be more like Him becomes ingrained in us.

> *Enter through the narrow gate. For wide is the gate and broad is the road that leads to destruction, and many enter through it. But small is the gate and narrow the road that leads to life, and only a few find it. Matthew 7: 13-14 (NIV)*

Day 67

ENERGY LEAK

We all have a limited amount of time and energy to expend. When we allow the past to steal from our energy store, we are left with a deficit to fulfill our needs for the day.

Energy leaks can be a result of the simplest things such as the laundry basket full of clothes that you remind yourself daily to be put away, but rather than getting it done, you expend the same amount of energy or more thinking about it the next day.

The energy leaks that steal the *greatest* amount of energy come from those things that are more difficult to manage, like the unpleasant things of our past. While we may not forget the things of our past, leaving the door open to it will drain us of our energy. Doing what is necessary to close the door to your past allows you to focus all your energy on the present.

At one point in my life, I found it very difficult to remove someone from my life with whom I had such a close connection. So, after ending an unhealthy intimate relationship, I tried to manage a friendship. But having to "manage" it was stealing my energy. Continued communication required that I expend energy trying to say and do the right things that wouldn't offend him. It required a lot of energy that I needed to spend elsewhere.

When the day finally came that I was able to completely remove him from my life it was bittersweet. I wanted things to end with both of us wishing each other well but he *wasn't* capable of that. However, I found peace and acceptance through the realization that I was expending energy on something that had no purpose whatsoever for my future. It was then that I fully committed to plug the "energy leak" and never allow it to steal my time and energy again.

Unproductive uses of our energy will leave us with a deficit to accomplish our tasks at hand. Don't allow your past to consume any amount of energy by dwelling there. Use the failures of your past to build a better future and expend your energy in that direction.

Jesus said to him, "no one who puts his hand to the plow and looks back is fit for the kingdom of God."
Luke 9:62 (ESV)

Day 68

INVALIDATION

I've done some study on the unhealthy need for attention and validation sometimes seen in adults. This can usually be traced back to childhood issues. While it's not healthy to live with a fear that we won't be validated, there is a healthy attention and validation of our emotions needed as part of a healthy relationship.

Psychologists define invalidation as "the process of denying, rejecting, or dismissing someone's feelings" and say it's a very damaging form of emotional abuse. Although there are intentional efforts made to devalue another person's feelings, oftentimes as well-intentioned as it may seem, we invalidate someone else's feelings in the process of trying to make them feel better, by insinuating that what they are going through is not as bad as they sense it to be. This sends the message that their feelings do not matter, or they are inaccurate.

There are also nonverbal forms of this abuse like giving someone the silent treatment. This basically tells the other person that when you don't agree with their feelings, they are not important enough to be heard. It is not our place to judge someone else's feelings. Whether or not we agree with them is beside the point. We do not have to agree with another person's feelings to validate them.

I consider attention and validation as key components of communication. When we validate someone's feelings, we are attentive to and accepting of their emotional state of being. The Bible tells us in Proverbs 18:17 (ESV), "The one who states his case first seems right until the other comes and examines him."

Listening and trying to understand the other person's perspective shows that you care and are willing to hear them out, whether you agree or not. When we become emotionally aware of each other's feelings, this results in better communication. This awareness does not mean that we are changing our position on the matter, but reflecting back how the other person is feeling shows that we understand. And it validates their right to have those feelings. This is an important component to work on for a healthy relationship.

If one gives an answer before he hears, it is his folly and shame. Proverbs 18:13 (ESV)

Day 69

THE ENEMY

We have likely all felt surrounded by the heaviness of this world at some point in our lives. But when the enemy tries to attack your mind, remember the battle has already been won. I heard Pastor Steven Furtick say, "The enemy uses the heaviest artillery on the people who are carrying the greatest purpose. If a lot is coming against you that means God has put a lot in you."

The Bible tells us that there is a table prepared for us in the presence of our enemies (Psalms 23:5). There is a song that says so beautifully, "It's Your body and Your blood You shed for me, this is how I fight my battles." It goes on to say, "It may look like I'm surrounded but I'm surrounded by You" and, "My weapons are praise and thanksgiving."

The enemy wants to use our time walking through difficulties to break us down. But instead of just surviving through the storm, if we allow Him to, God will use it for something great. We can harden our hearts or become bitter toward others because of the things that we have gone through…or we can use them as a place for learning how to love the way God calls us to love.

We are to love not only our friends but also our enemies. I carry this verse in my heart as a reminder that I don't hold onto anger when others hurt me because the Bible says, "For our struggle is not against flesh and blood, but against the rulers, against the authorities, against the powers of this dark world and against spiritual forces of evil in the heavenly realms" (Ephesians 6:12 NIV).

When we walk through the difficult times in our lives, we are walking towards our future purpose. Though I got pregnant at 17, divorced after 27 years, and made some bad choices, this does not change the purpose that God has for my life. God didn't disqualify His purpose for me because I messed up; instead, He is using it for my good and His glory because I'm called according to His purpose. God is still there working in the midst of all your mess and if you're willing, you can choose to allow God to turn that mess into your message.

Be sober-minded; be watchful. Your adversary the devil prowls around like a roaring lion, seeking someone to devour. 1 Peter 5:8 (ESV)

Here's a song I'd like to share with you – Surrounded (Fight My Battles):
https://youtu.be/nWmjpF613y4

Day 70

EVALUATING THE SELF

When you're still wanting to reach out for someone or something that is not good for you, ask yourself what it is that you are looking to gain from this. I had to evaluate myself and ask what I needed from an unhealthy relationship with someone that I couldn't seem to detach from. What was this relationship giving me?

I was showered with attention, a feeling of love, and my every need was catered to. But the truth was, I was feeding upon this love and attention from a man who also betrayed me, tried to exploit me, lied compulsively to me, and consistently turned the tables to blame *everything* on me while he played the victim. I came to understand that not only could my appetite for love and attention *not* be satisfied by such a relationship but that the unhealthy behaviors of others were not a reflection of me or my worth.

The only unhealthy behaviors you are responsible for are your own. The truth is that the betrayal I continued to subject myself to, could not be blamed on anyone else but myself; it was an indication of my own issues. I needed to learn to love and take care of myself. This came through my personal and spiritual growth and recovery journey which led me to understand that there was only One who could satiate this desire I had to be loved. The love we find in relationships is just an added bonus.

Are you looking for someone else to make you feel loved or to take care of you? Taking care of ourselves in every aspect of our lives – whether it be emotional or physical health, fitness, spirituality or any number of other things, is when we are truly loving ourselves and capable of attracting a healthy love from others. Understand who you are. I am a child of the Almighty King which means I am a Princess! Who are you?

> *See what great love the Father has lavished on us,*
> *that we should be called children of God! And that*
> *is what we are! The reason the world does not*
> *know us is that it did not know him.*
> *1 John 3:1 (NIV)*

Day 71

IMPOSTOR SYNDROME

Impostor syndrome is a psychological process of doubting your skills and achievements and having a fear of being "exposed" as a fraud. Prior to my personal growth and recovery work, I tried to make sure what people saw from the outside was me having it all together. I worked very hard not to let the damaged pieces of what was inside, crack through for others to see. But this ultimately always led to an underlying belief that I had deceived people into thinking I was better than I was, so I always held myself to a very high standard to keep up with this persona.

When God guided me in the direction of sharing my journey of personal growth and recovery publicly, I questioned who I was that I had *any* knowledge to give to others. I felt like I had to hide the fact that I wasn't as well-versed in the bible as I would like to be, that I didn't have it all together, or that my heart was still hurt by things from my past.

When others began to lean into what I was sharing and find encouragement through it, that imposter syndrome viciously kicked in. I was slammed with feelings of inadequacy and the enemy wanted to disable me by that! I began to put a lot of pressure on myself to make others believe that I had it all together and it began to interfere with my time with God. But the truth is when it became apparent or actually when I allowed it to become transparent that I didn't have it all together; and that this was part of my story for God to use, what a huge relief it was!

> I was slammed with feelings of inadequacy and the enemy wanted to disable me by that!

Don't allow impostor syndrome to stand between you and what God has called you to do. You *are* good enough and you are able – because it's not about you, it's about God working *through* you.

I encourage you to read Luke 5 as Jesus called His disciples to cast their nets again. Remember what happened after the bible verse below, they caught such a large number of fish their nets began to break!

Simon answered, "Master we have worked hard all night and haven't caught anything. But because you say so I will let down the nets."
Luke 5:5 (NIV)

Day 72

ENABLING PAIN

Engaging in a relationship with someone who has consistently shown behaviors that are not healthy and is making no steady effort towards true change, essentially *enables* that person to continue in the unhealthy state they are in.

I was encouraged by the wisdom that came from my recovery coach: That just the same as my leaving allowed me an opportunity to evaluate myself and choose to get well, it also did the same for the other person. And, whether the other person chose to get well or not, was a choice only that person could make.

I couldn't quite figure out why my relationship with this person was so important for me to succeed at. He had some good qualities and showered me with attention but at the expense of me overlooking his compulsive lying, alcohol abuse, emotional instability, and deceitfulness. This was a character flaw that I had to address *in myself*.

My spirit was *never* at peace. I had to find a way to let go and then trust that God would meet us both where we were as I did. Through the process of letting go of this relationship and my choice to get well, I realized that I had become enmeshed in the relationship and that I often *pitied* him rather than *loving* him.

Oh, how I wanted to rescue him and make everything better, not only for him but selfishly for myself. When I accepted that I couldn't make him well nor was it my job to "fix" him I went through a process of denial and anger. In the end, God gave me the strength and the wisdom to detach in a loving way. I was hopeful that he could do the same and that he'd wish me well, but he wasn't able to do that. As I struggled to accept his disapproval of my decision, this revealed another character flaw that had to be addressed within myself.

The journey to healing is not easy, but God is always faithful to show up in a big way. The pain you endure through the process of healing leads to a much better place versus the pain that is never-ending by staying where you are.

Good and upright is the Lord; therefore he instructs sinners in the way. He guides the humble in what is right and teaches them his way. All the ways of the Lord are loving and faithful toward those who keep the demands of his covenant.
Psalms 25: 8-10 (NIV)

Day 73

LOVE ADDICTION

The eye-opening knowledge I gained on the topic of love addiction and love avoidance led me to understand that while finding love is a wonderful part of life for emotionally healthy people, for others, love is a source of addiction that interferes with their ability to have a healthy relationship.

A love addict has an inability to relate to their partner in a non-addictive way. Their dysfunctional way of relating in relationships and their constant need for reassurance to feel loved is usually rooted in unresolved childhood issues. They feel empty without someone to love and take care of them. They often find themselves in a co-addicted relationship or one with a love-avoidant partner.

When a relationship exists between two love addicts it becomes obsessive, intense and they become completely enmeshed with each other, sometimes to the extent of excluding friends, family, and children.

Even when a relationship exists between a love addict and a love avoidant, this intensity is present as they often switch roles. For example, when a love addict feels drained from trying to be who their partner wants them to be, they can take on characteristics of the love avoidant, or when the love avoidant realizes they aren't being pursued, their feelings of abandonment are triggered and they may begin to mimic the role of the love addict.

A love addict finds it nearly impossible to leave a relationship because they have become dependent. They feel like the relationship is the only thing that can satisfy their need for love or their feelings of emptiness and their tolerance of unhealthy behaviors increases.

Unfortunately, anger and resentment follow, which often results in toxic fighting. This addictive process can take control of a person's life just the same as *any other* addiction. Attempts at overcoming it may repeatedly fail. They feel trapped, unable to leave, and yet not wanting to stay. They may even lose most of their ability to truly feel emotion.

The withdrawal symptoms can be so intense that they are nearly impossible to fight. It is like a drug and making that connection with the other person is the only thing that seems to satisfy the "fix" they crave. When they return to the other person, the cycle repeats.

> It is like a drug and making that connection is the only thing that seems to satisfy that "fix"…

It is a long, difficult journey through recovery to recognize and resolve these issues. But it's important to understand that love shouldn't hurt, it shouldn't be miserable, lonely, or make us unhappy. It's only by becoming aware and understanding this process that a love addict can change the way they think, behave and relate to people and have a relationship that is truly free of dysfunction.

> *And after you have suffered a little while, the God of all grace, who has called you to his eternal glory in Christ, will himself restore, confirm, strengthen, and establish you. 1 Peter 5:10 (ESV)*

Day 74

LOVE AVOIDANT

Similar to a love addict, a love avoidant enters relationships with dysfunctional issues. In the childhood of a love avoidant, the role of the caretaker was often assumed by the child – so as adults, they feel it's their job to take care of their partner. However, they fear enmeshment, so they subconsciously don't allow themselves to become emotionally attached.

Love avoidants have learned the art of charm and seduction to hide their fears. They become master manipulators of their partner's feelings, but behind the scenes, they focus on addictions outside of the relationship such as compulsive sexuality, alcohol abuse, or a host of other addictions to fuel and satisfy their feelings of emptiness, fear of abandonment, and fear of enmeshment. Through their charming, seductive, love bombing ways, a love avoidant often attracts a love addict who requires reassurance to feel loved and who tries to enmesh with their partner.

When the love avoidant feels this kind of pressure, their fears are triggered, and they turn to their addictions outside of the relationship. Neither a love addict nor a love avoidant has healthy self-love, so they look for an intimate relationship to make them feel loved.

In the same way a love addict can switch roles and take on characteristics of a love avoidant, when a love avoidant feels as though they aren't being pursued, it triggers their fear of abandonment and they may begin to take on characteristics of a love addict. This type of relationship creates a constant push-pull dynamic that becomes obsessive and intense. It's only through a willingness to acknowledge the issues and commit to doing the hard work of recovery that initiates change, can a love avoidant ever have a healthy relationship.

> *No temptation has overtaken you that is not common to man. God is faithful, and he will not let you be tempted beyond your ability, but with the temptation he will also provide the way of escape, that you may be able to endure it.*
> *1 Corinthians 10:13 (ESV)*

Day 75

ENMESHMENT

Enmeshment trauma occurs in childhood when a child loses their sense of self, trying to tend to the emotional needs of an adult, which are instead meant to be met by another adult. For example, a divorced mother may look to her male child to fill the emotional void in her life and may want her son to take the "man's place" in the home. As adults in romantic relationships, they often become love avoidants as they rebel against enmeshment but oddly attract partners who seek to enmesh. The love addict seeks to enmesh with this person whom they see as a fantasy hero who will take care of them.

Becoming enmeshed with someone can cause you to begin neglecting other relationships outside of your focused relationship, and your feelings of well-being become contingent upon it. When you are enmeshed with someone, you have no clear boundaries of where your self ends and the other person begins.

Enmeshment leads to feeling that the other person's emotions are your own. You feel an excessive need to take care of a relationship and avoid any disagreements and you may feel lonely unless you're in the presence of the relationship. You have intense irrational desires to connect and a lack of self-love that manifests itself in compulsive behaviors and intense emotions of fear, anger, and extreme positive and negative interactions.

In healthy relationships, feelings of tension, anxiety, uncertainty, and discontentment are not there when you're apart. Healthy relationships require space and time apart, not rescuing and being rescued. That's enmeshment and the relationship can't grow in this tangled state. Shifting your focus to recovering from unhealthy patterns and old wounds brings healing and new ways to relate to others.

Out of my distress I called on the Lord; the Lord answered me and set me free. Psalm 118:5 (ESV)

Day 76

WHO I AM

Through the process of my personal and spiritual growth and recovery journey, God placed a desire in my heart to reach others who are suffering where I once was. When God calls you to do something, you can consider it done as you follow where He leads. We can walk in His favor and like the bible says He will give us new strength to grow and not become weary, to walk and not faint.

I knew that where my spirit was leading me was a "God thing" because it wasn't really something I wanted to do. It felt difficult, uncomfortable, and unfamiliar. But when I didn't see the support of some family and friends which I expected, I questioned if maybe it wasn't God leading me to do this, and I considered turning back. But God was faithful in continuing to lead me and give me the wisdom to understand that it wasn't about my family and friends, it went far beyond that.

Promotion comes from God. It's never about the future version of who you are with God. It's about where you are now and how God wants to use you here, at this moment. We cannot give away our power and base our future on our expectations for approval and support from others. When Jesus returned to his hometown of Nazareth, He was rejected. The people there were so familiar with Him as Mary's son – the carpenter, that they couldn't see Him for who He truly was.

There will be people who are just too busy with their own lives to be part of yours, people who don't like you, people who won't support you, people who only see your mistakes, and people who will never see you for anyone else, other than who they think you are. Regardless of what others see, when you refuse to allow yourself to become so comfortable with where you are, that you can't see where God is leading you, that's when God will use you! It's not for us to know the time or place of God's plan but to follow where He leads.

We don't know what's coming next, or where we are going. Sometimes we may feel like we don't even know what we are doing half the time. But God orders our steps, not our friends, family, or anyone else.

When God says to do something, do you listen and promptly follow, or do you wait for your friends, family, or others to guide you? We must choose our battles, and waging war against what God has called me to do is not one I want to fight. So, I ask the Lord to remove my need for approval from anyone but Him!

We are going to mess up sometimes and say or do the wrong things, but God has already gone before you, He is walking beside you, and He is even following behind you, picking up all the pieces that you drop. His strength is made perfect in your weakness. Come into agreement with God's calling on your life and trust that He will lead you. As I stand in His presence, I understand that He is God and I am not. He is God and I am Kim.

> *The steps of a man are established by the Lord, when he delights in his way; though he fall, he shall not be cast headlong, for the Lord upholds his hand. Psalm 37: 23-24 (ESV)*

Day 77

ABOVE AND BEYOND

"Above and beyond" are words that I feel are attached to my being. In my career, going above and beyond was awarded with promotions. In school, my going above and beyond was awarded with other types of recognition, and so on.

I came to a point where I found myself justifiably needing a break, but somehow, I couldn't allow myself to take a break. I felt that if I stopped, I would never gain traction, or possibly never start again.

The pressure I was feeling came from the thought of allowing myself to "give up" which had never been in my DNA. But during that time, it felt like it would be a relief to just stop, not do anything, and just hide! Yet the fear of going back to what awaited felt meaningless, it felt like a failure and pointless for what I had achieved up to that point and where I wanted to go. I eventually discovered that what was waiting had I stopped producing, were all the unhealed issues from my past.

It was through reflecting back over my life that I realized that I only felt I was at my best when I was striving for something whether it was my degree, a career, a finished project, or satisfying a relationship. Those were the times I looked my best, dressed my best, and acted my best at the part. When I came to this point where I wasn't feeling my best but still acting out these motions, I knew something was wrong. The words I always spoke, "no matter how you feel, get up, dress up, and show up" – seemed to be working *against* me.

What I came to understand is that I was trying to work, work, work to move ahead of my past because the more I focused on the future the further away my past became. But the unresolved issues were still following me *everywhere* I went. I couldn't outwork nor outrun the piercing pain of my past.

> But the unresolved issues were still following me everywhere I went. I couldn't outwork nor outrun the piercing pain of my past.

I was always excited about what my future held, but I was never satisfied with what I had achieved. Nothing ever seemed to be good enough – because my healing had to come *first*. Before I could ever be a good leader in business, a mentor to others, or a partner in a relationship, I had to let go of the work that I was trying to do to outrun my past and let God do the work in me that needed to be done.

> *Therefore, if anyone is in Christ, he is a new creation. The old has passed away; behold, the new has come. 2 Corinthians 5: 17 (ESV)*

Day 78

THE STORM

*I*n the same way that it would be nearly impossible to fix your home in the midst of a storm, it's also very unlikely that you can heal emotionally during the midst of one – so taking some time to withdraw can be beneficial.

When you're withdrawing from something or someone in life that has harmed you, giving yourself time can be healing. However, in the same way that it would be unrealistic to wait for time to fix the damage to your home from a storm, the rain of trials and suffering we face in life *can't* always be healed with time. Attention is often needed in the areas of spiritual growth and recovery before healing can occur.

When storms come in our relationships it can feel devastating, especially if we are looking for our worth from that connection. I once tried to find my worth in a man who placed me up on a pedestal and catered to my every desire, only to knock me down repeatedly.

Looking to find your worth in someone else will cause you to run back into a storm *repeatedly*. This is something that time alone won't heal. We must be intentional about pursuing inner healing. When you are spiritually unhealthy, that is whom you will attract, and whom you will be attracted to.

When the rain and wind from the storms of life come, as devastating as it can seem, we have the power to choose whether we continue to dwell in the midst of devastation, or pick up the pieces and build something new. God will bring purpose to the storm if we allow Him, and when we gain incredible wisdom from it all, as the old Milli Vanilli song says, we can "blame it on the rain."

> *By wisdom a house is built, and by understanding it is established; through knowledge its rooms are filled with rare and beautiful treasures.*
> *Proverbs 24:3-4 (ESV)*

Day 79

SITTING WITH GOD

*I*n the midst of our trials and struggles, God is waiting for us to bring them to Him. Recently, I was struggling with something that felt so much bigger than me. I seemed to be facing a giant and it was just little ole me trying to fight the battle.

As I continued to pray about the situation, during one of my meditations I had a vision of a mother crossing the street with her child. She asks the child to wait while she steps ahead to see that the way is safe. Then, she calls the child to her and they hold hands while crossing together. Finally, she looks behind and sees the child has dropped things, so she goes behind to pick them up. At that moment, the giant I felt like I was facing, suddenly dissipated. I gained a new clarity. I knew God was reminding me that He had already gone *before* me and made the way. He also walks *beside* me through it all and follows up *behind* me cleaning up all my mess.

When the struggle felt so much bigger than me, it was. When it seemed like it was just little ole me trying to face this giant, it was. That was the struggle. God had given me an assignment to carry out but rather than sitting with Him and allowing Him to lead me, I tried to take control. I neglected my time with Him to finish the task within my time frame. What I was facing really was so much bigger than me and it could only be fulfilled by God through me.

I'm so thankful that even through my mess of vanity and pride that tries to creep in, God follows behind me, cleans up my mess, and uses me anyway! Like the song says, "He doesn't need me but somehow He still wants me." Have you been struggling with something and feel like you're fighting the battle alone? The solution lies in your answer to this, my friend: Are you spending quality time with God in prayer and His word?

You will keep in perfect peace those whose minds are steadfast, because they trust in you. Isaiah 26:3 (NIV)

Here's a song I'd like to share with you – Control: https://youtu.be/kFfztu8-bBQ

Day 80

GOD'S FAVOR

I named 2020 my year of abundant blessings and despite what we all know of 2020, it was just that! I expected and declared God's favor in my life. Things may be hard, they may be uncomfortable, you may be feeling overwhelmed or inadequate, but God!

Nothing you are facing is bigger than God. He has a plan and He is waiting for you to allow Him to finish what He set out to accomplish in you. What's ahead of you is far greater than what is behind you. God has already gone ahead of you and paved the way.

When you feel you aren't good enough, but God! God is walking with you and working through you. When you mess up, but God! He's walking behind you and cleaning it up. When you expect support from family and friends that you don't get, but God! It's not about you, it's about allowing God to use you as his vessel.

So, no matter how hard it may be, no matter how much you mess up, no matter who doesn't support you, but God! He is there every step of the way.

When you step out in faith, following where God has led you, but you face difficulties – that does not mean that you can't hear God, or you heard him wrong. This is often the enemy trying to creep in and stop you in your tracks. He plants seeds of doubt in our mind, but we are to take every thought captive and make it obedient to Christ. We are to speak those things that aren't as if they are.

Don't allow anyone else to create your story except God. You may have suffered through so many things in life that have brought you to this point, but then God! Your story is the road between the suffering of your past and someone else's victory and healing!

God is in me! I walk in God's favor and I will finish with His favor forgetting those things that are behind me and focusing forward. You, too, can walk and finish with God's favor. We can take God at His Word no matter how it looks or feels.

> *(As it is written, I have made you a father of many nations,) before him whom he believed, even God, who quickeneth the dead, and calleth those things which be not as though they were.*
> *Romans 4:17 (KJV)*

Day 81

PERFECTIONISM

rior to my personal growth journey, I was never able to label it but I saw it at its best, or I should say, its worst, through me, and that was *perfectionism*. In our careers, making mistakes can cost a lot of money, among other things, so it's important to be detailed and do a great job. Most of us strive to do our best in our personal lives as well. However, perfectionism creates an obsession that can wreak havoc on our lives.

Striving for growth and improvement is an attainable goal but striving for perfection that can never be achieved, is exhausting. Perfectionists are very hard on themselves and find it difficult to accept anything less than perfection. A minor mistake may lead to weeks of criticizing themselves.

Their feelings are rooted in the belief that doing *everything* perfectly will bring them great satisfaction, and result in the approval and appreciation of others. They work obsessively to gain fulfillment in their finished projects, only to be met with feelings that it wasn't good enough. Perfectionism associates accomplishments with personal worth and it's never satiated, so it always requires an onward motion towards achievement.

Reflecting back over my life, I can see many areas where perfectionism inflicted a great amount of unnecessary stress. One of the more recent experiences was when I decided to return to school for my accounting degree. I completed this four-year degree in less than two and a half years while also working full time. In the meantime, I had this belief that anything less than an "A" was not good enough.

I remember proudly sharing my grades and GPA with others, yet when I walked across the stage for my diploma, I didn't feel satisfied with my accomplishment. I recall spending days on a project that took others just a couple of hours – because my work was never good enough to satisfy me. I received comments from professors saying things like, "this is the best critique of this article I've ever seen," and they even asked permission to use my work in their collection of pieces. But no compliment *ever* satisfied me, it served only to make me work harder, fearing that I would let someone down the next time.

While I couldn't label perfectionism then, I've since had to work very hard at surrendering the heavy burden of expecting perfection from myself that can never be attained in this life. God does not want us to carry the weight of our burdens upon ourselves. He asks us to bring everything to Him so He can give us rest.

> *Then Jesus said, "Come to me, all you who are weary and carry heavy burdens, and I will give you rest. Take my yoke upon you. Let me teach you, because I am humble and gentle at heart, and you will find rest for your souls. For my yoke is easy to bear, and the burden I give you is light."*
> *Matthew 11:28-30 (NLT)*

Day 82

NARCISSISM

Narcissism is a personality disorder with traits ranging from chronic boredom that requires excessive attention and admiration from others, to superficial relationships shaped by an inability to empathize. A narcissist's inability to empathize sadly limits their ability to love. They see others as possessions. However, not recognizing the fragile and vulnerable narcissist who shows emotion can be the most detrimental, as their victims are left feeling absolutely no closure from the relationship – because they are unable to find the truth of who the person truly was.

Narcissists have mastered the art of disguise to get their needs met. Like a chameleon, they can alter themselves almost instantly to seem like your perfect partner. They study every detail of your being and then mirror it back, leading you to believe in a special bond that no one else has ever shared.

They are extroverts and often have a large group of friends; however, all their relationships are specifically to benefit their fantasy image of success, power, beauty, and love. Anything that contradicts this imagined reality gets justified and rationalized, sometimes to the point of acting out in rage. In romantic relationships, it seems like a fairytale beginning. They love-bomb their primary source of "narcissistic supply" to the point that their victims feel they have found the most amazing person ever. But behind the scenes lies and betrayal await.

When you try to leave, you'll be pursued relentlessly – yet this is not about feeling love for you. The loss of a narcissist's main supply is a hit to their ego and the fantasy image they try to uphold. When their attempts to keep you fail, they feel shame and abandonment so they become enraged and try harder to prove their worth. A narcissist will continue to return to each of their relationships for "supply" until it's no longer provided, or it no longer benefits them. When their main source of supply is no longer available, they easily find a new primary source elsewhere.

It's difficult to explain in such few words the trauma associated with an encounter with a narcissist. A core trait of every narcissist will be an inability to take responsibility for their actions. In the rare event that they do, it is accompanied by excuses to justify themselves. Their weapon of "crazy"-making, blaming, justifying, lies, and betrayal will leave you questioning what is real versus a façade.

Escaping a narcissist is difficult and the recovery process from the trauma is intense. It's so important to recognize what's broken in you, so you can find healing, protect yourself and attract healthier relationships. If this resonates with you, ask God to help you surrender the person and the relationship to Him, and then focus on addressing what needs healing within yourself.

*I the Lord search the heart and examine the mind,
to reward each person according to their conduct,
according to what their deeds deserve.
Jeremiah 17:10 (NIV)*

Day 83

"CRAZY"-MAKING

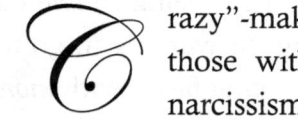razy"-making behavior is a tactic used by those with personality disorders such as narcissism, psychopathy, and sociopathy. According to many sources, these disorders of self-esteem have overlapping characteristics, with the main difference being that a narcissist will feel guilt and shame, although it's out of their fear of being viewed by others in a negative light, whereas a psychopath or sociopath doesn't feel guilt, shame or remorse. Their "crazy"-making behavior leaves you full of doubt and concern that you might be crazy or imagining things.

The weapon of "crazy"-making behavior begins with the ability to confuse you with a cycle of exhilaration and desolation. For example, when a narcissist feels low on "narcissistic supply" rather than seeing their elation you may see them vulnerable, crying, and apologizing. You may hear their sad story about how they've never loved anyone like you, along with how badly their ex treated them, or their issues of abandonment from childhood. These are all manipulation tactics.

Their story causes you to see them as a victim who needs you, and the thought of abandoning the relationship inflicts feelings of guilt. You will begin to blame yourself for every situation, you'll be groomed to believe that you over-analyze everything and that nobody thinks about things the way *you* do. You stay in a state of cognitive dissonance, unable to determine who this person really is, one moment being showered with affection, crying, apologizing, or wanting to go to counseling, and the next moment being faced with *more* lies and deception.

Remember this "crazy"-making behavior is a weapon used by those with personality disorders, and it is a form of emotional abuse. Your brain becomes addicted to the cycles of highs and lows, and your decision making becomes irrational – as you become increasingly tolerant of inappropriate behavior. In the same way that recovering from alcohol or drugs requires abstinence, **no contact** is the way to begin overcoming this type of abuse. You must surrender the person and the relationship to God and commit to living by faith and not feelings.

Whoever trusts in his own mind is a fool, but he who walks in wisdom will be delivered.
Proverbs 28:26 (ESV)

Day 84

GRACE AND GRATITUDE

When the coronavirus first took the media by storm and the effects it would have on our families and our economies were anticipated, some continued to have a light heart amidst the news we faced, while others carried a heavy burden. We didn't know what the days ahead held, but when do we ever?

As Christians, what we know with certainty is that God is still in control even when we don't like what's happening and we are to give thanks in all circumstances. Does this actually mean giving thanks for a pandemic or the death of a loved one? Of course not. But amidst the circumstance, we give thanks for God's grace that – as Christians – we know is new every morning and is given proportionately to our needs.

The Bible tells us in Ephesians 4:7 (NIV), "But to each one of us grace has been given as Christ apportioned it." What that means is, for example, when you see a parent who has lost a child and you can't fathom how they are making it through, well that's because you haven't needed that grace. God has met them where they're at with what they need.

When my mom was in the hospital on life support, I saw others go about their daily lives while she was fighting for hers, and while I seemed to just be surviving one moment to the next. What I wanted in those moments was for my mom to wake up. But what I was given was the grace to make it through each moment that she didn't. What I wanted, walking away from the hospital that last time was to have her walking alongside me. But what I was given was the grace to find the strength to walk away with the most amazing gratitude in ways I'll have to share another time and a vision of her walking away with angels on streets made of gold.

In every circumstance, God gives us grace and we are to give thanks. I am grateful for all the people who share messages of encouragement and prayers with me through difficult times. I am grateful to be able to rest in my cozy home if I'm not feeling well. I continue to find so much to be grateful for in the midst of a storm, and do you know what? When you practice gratitude, it starts to show up naturally. What attitude will you choose when you face a difficult season?

Rejoice always, pray continually, give thanks in all circumstances; for this is God's will for you in Christ Jesus. 1 Thessalonians 5:18 (NIV)

Day 85

SEX

*R*ecently, as I drove across the lake, admiring its beauty, I thought about how something so beautiful that brings so much fun and pleasure can be so dangerous when used inappropriately. It's funny, but my thoughts at that moment related it to the beauty, fun, and pleasure of sex that when used outside of the purpose God created it turns into something detrimental to our spirit, soul, and body. Sex is a physical act that binds us emotionally. In almost any relationship that ends, we can identify the most hurt from a soul tie that has emotionally bound us to that person.

As a young girl, I always said I would wait until marriage. What I realize now is that those words were more ingrained in me from my upbringing than they were a conscious decision, as I found myself pregnant at 17. After ending a 27-year marriage I moved on quickly to the next relationship and once again sex took priority. I knew waiting until marriage was what God instructed, but I wanted what I wanted. I'm forgiven of my sins after all, right?

What I came to understand was that among the reasons for God creating sex specifically for marriage was to protect us from harm. God knows that this physical act binds us emotionally and that sex outside of marriage creates an ungodly soul tie that causes extreme heartache and makes it difficult to disconnect from someone. We can take back and mend our heart, or replace physical things that were lost, but in walking away from someone to whom we have given something we can't get back, we lose a piece of ourselves forever and we remain connected to that person.

I heard one of my favorite Pastors, Steven Furtick, say that somebody once asked him why he didn't talk like where he came from, referring to his accent. He said he told her she was a *child of God* and asked why she didn't talk like where she came from, i.e. God. I started to question why I didn't act like where I came from. I have royal blood. I am a princess of the Almighty King. Only one, the one whom God has prepared for you is deserving of your whole royal self. Until you find that one, let others come and go without losing a piece of yourself in the process.

Flee from sexual immorality. Every other sin a person commits is outside the body, but the sexually immoral person sins against his own body. Or do you not know that your body is a temple of the Holy Spirit within you, who you have from God? You are not your own, for you were bought with a price. So glorify God in your body.
1 Corinthians 6:18-20 (ESV)

Day 86

ABANDONMENT

It is a basic human need to connect with people. This is seen from birth when a child is placed on the mother's chest. Fear of abandonment often stems from a traumatic childhood experience and can lead to many different unhealthy behaviors. Those who suffer from abandonment issues lean toward one extreme or another from thoughts of "please don't leave me" to subconsciously pushing people away and not allowing themselves to get close to anyone.

Because we are hardwired to recreate childhood experiences, we are drawn to the same type of relationships that we had in childhood because they are familiar. People-pleasing, putting others' needs ahead of your own, insecurity, trust issues, and fear of disapproval are a few ways that *fear of abandonment* manifests itself.

In romantic relationships, abandonment issues can sometimes lead to affairs because the person fears losing their current relationship, so they keep one on the side. Other ways this fear can manifest itself are: holding onto and repeatedly returning to a relationship, immediately moving on to a new relationship when one ends, or pushing away relationships out of fear of rejection.

If any of these resonate with you, invite God in to show you areas where healing needs to be done. Commit to doing some work in recovery that will lead to a better understanding of the ways in which, as a child, a primary caregiver may have unknowingly contributed to your fear of abandonment. Learning to love yourself and acknowledging that your past does not have to affect your future relationships can encourage healthier decisions and lead to feelings of trust rather than fear.

And those who know your name put their trust in you, for you, O Lord, have not forsaken those who seek you. Psalms 9:10 (ESV)

Day 87

SINCERITY

When we encounter a breach of trust, we always see a breakdown in some core area such as capability, reliability, or sincerity. Addressing these core areas prior to determining someone trustworthy will save you a lot of heartaches. For so long I placed my trust in others until they gave me a reason not to, but I learned that trust is something earned not given.

Sometimes when our trust has been betrayed, we vow to ourselves that we are not going to connect with anyone again. But this is not the way God designed us to be. We all have a desire to connect with others. So, learning to recognize sincerity prior to placing our trust in someone is important. We must evaluate if a person is capable of delivering on what they promise.

For example, when a promise is made yet broken, finding the root issue to determine why that person was unable to carry through on their promise is necessary. Repeated broken promises show a lack of reliability and if a person is capable of following through on their promises yet lacks reliability in doing so, then it's safe to conclude that their efforts are not sincere but rather an attempt to gain your support.

When sincerity is lacking, a person will tell you what they think you want to hear, versus what they actually think or what their true intentions are. This is deceit and what I believe to be the root issue of untrustworthiness that brings the most heartache. God places a high regard on sincerity, and it is free from deceit and hypocrisy. While we can never be certain of someone's intentions or sincerity, it is never hidden from God and we can place our trust in Him to lead us into what is true and right.

The aim of our charge is love that issues from a pure heart and a good conscience and a sincere faith.
1 Timothy 1:5 (ESV)

Day 88

EMOTIONAL SOBRIETY

Are you conscious of your emotions? Do you allow them to control your actions? Our emotions can be a barrier to logical thinking. When I first learned of emotional sobriety, it was explained to me as the period of time between experiencing the trigger and reacting to it. But how do you achieve emotional sobriety?

I found that learning the skill of "observing" can lead to emotional sobriety. Yet, learning this skill can be tricky. The true tool of *observing* is to watch and experience from a detached place, taking inventory of the facts without reacting to them or trying to change them.

When we create division between ourselves and our emotions and learn to focus our energy on *observing the facts* without interference, we are observing from a detached place. When we observe the facts that surround our emotions as something apart from ourselves instead of attaching ourselves to what is happening or what we think should be happening, this leads to emotional sobriety.

When we achieve emotional sobriety, we allow ourselves to sit in the discomfort of our emotions rather than react to the discomfort. We no longer allow our actions or our wellbeing to be dependent on how we think things should be. Things will not always conform to our expectations, so rather than allowing our emotions to control us, we can find emotional sobriety through letting go of those things that are out of our control and happening outside of ourselves. Reacting to the discomfort of our emotions can lead to unhealthy behaviors, but learning to observe from a detached place leads to growth and emotional maturity.

> *Therefore, preparing your minds for action, and being sober-minded, set your hope fully on the grace that will be brought to you at the revelation of Jesus Christ 1 Peter 1:3 (ESV)*

Day 89

AUTHENTICITY

Has anyone ever assumed that your joy, your faith, or your success came from never having endured hardships? Have you ever looked at someone else and assumed that their anger, lack of faith, or their mess was a result of anything other than the hardships they had endured? Well, you know what they say when you assume.

I heard T.D. Jakes say, "Those that God is going to anoint the most, he always crushes the most severely."

It's how we handle hardships that determines our success versus our mess, faith versus doubt, and joy versus sorrow. As Christians, we find joy in spite of our circumstances, faith even when things look hopeless, and success in walking through our failures one step at a time. We know that whatever situation we are faced with, God is with us.

When King Nebuchadnezzar had Shadrach, Meshach, and Abednego thrown into the blazing furnace for worshiping God, he witnessed a fourth man in the fire with them. It was God! Even when God does not remove us from our circumstances, He is there with us.

Sometimes, as well-intentioned as it may seem, we turn others away from Christianity with hypocrisy or a "holier than thou" attitude. We hide our true selves and what we have been through, and sometimes still struggle with. How can we inspire anyone else of God's love and his blessings if we are not sharing it? No one will see Christ through you until they see you!

Others can't see where you've been or what you've overcome until you share your authentic self. At that point, amidst your joy, faith, and success they can also see their own mess in you; they see their own doubt in you, and they see their own sorrow in you. But they also see something in you that they lack – they see the Spirit of God living in you.

As you make progress through your own journey, I hope you are encouraged to share your authenticity. It may be the difference between pointing someone to Christ and turning them away. As you share your story authentically, you give the glory to God, and others can see Him through you.

Then Nebuchadnezzar said, "Praise be to the God of Shadrach, Meshach and Abednego, who has sent his angel and rescues his servants! They trusted in him and defied the king's command and were willing to give up their lives rather than serve or worship any god except their own God."
Daniel 3:28 (NIV)

Day 90

POTENTIAL

As a very young toddler, my oldest daughter expressed her independence. She was a sweet, high-spirited little girl who took charge whether it was by climbing up on the counter to fix her own bowl of cereal or telling others how to do it. She was very "opinionated," always ready to argue her point. She had just turned two years old when I remember my mom telling her, "You have made a mess of Grandma's house" and hearing her reply, "This is not Grandma's house, this is Grandma's living room."

When her little sister came along, she knew just how to employ her to get exactly what she wanted. While some of these qualities could have been seen as rebellious or domineering, I saw them as great leadership skills. She was intelligent, a straight "A" student through high school for the most part, and I thought of all the things she had the potential to achieve with her courageous attitude. Possibly an attorney with her persistence and determination in proving her point, or a teacher since she knew just how to get others to do what she wanted.

My point is this: when you apply what you or others can sometimes see in a negative light to the right purpose in your life, you see potential. The same words that have the potential to silence your spirit are also the words that can motivate you toward your potential. There's a huge difference between falling short and stopping short. Some of us will never meet our potential because when we fall short, we stop short. Your potential is not the sum of all the times you fell short. Your potential is found in *not* stopping short.

I may fall short at times, but I keep pressing toward my God-given potential. God fills in the gaps to make me everything I'm not. In the mornings, ask God to lead and guide me through the day. Ask Him what He has in store for you. Then speak out loud with assurance, "Lord, whatever it is that awaits me today, I know You have gone before me and have seen what's ahead. You have walked my path, cleared the way, and will walk beside me every step of this day." When you are tempted to stop short, trust that God is leading and guiding you toward your potential and press on toward the mark of the high calling He has on your life.

I press toward the mark for the prize of the high calling of God in Christ Jesus. Philippians 3:14 (KJV

RECOMMENDED RESOURCES

Facing Love Addiction: https://amzn.to/3ae7zPb

Addiction to Love: https://amzn.to/2Z4laCf

A Hunger for Healing: https://amzn.to/2MTNIvE

Codependents Guide to the Twelve Steps: https://amzn.to/3717n3w

The Betrayal Bond: https://amzn.to/3a7aXuP

Whole Again: https://amzn.to/2LDZf1p

Psychopath free: https://amzn.to/374bdsF

Untangle: https://amzn.to/3jBZGpA

Beyond Boundaries: https://amzn.to/3rIEyRn

Boundaries in Dating: https://amzn.to/3p92KuB

Life and Recovery Coaching:

https://heidilemusic.com/vip-breakthrough-coaching-clients

KIMBERLY A. SANFORD

Kimberly is an advocate for personal and spiritual growth and recovery work. She brings her own growth and Christian perspective in these areas to her writing after the end of a 27-year marriage followed by a developing pattern of other unhealthy relationships.

In the midst of her journey to find healing from this cycle she began to practice principles that exemplified a restored state of being. She refers to her journey as a renovation process of the spirit, soul, and body relating it to a broken outdated structure being improved to a new-like state but not before uncovering some messy stuff hidden beneath the surface.

She embodies strength and courage in her writing as she passionately empowers others to identify and break free from unhealthy and toxic behaviors that bind in a seemingly unbreakable grip and find the freedom to reach their best self.

Kim has two beautiful daughters and four amazing grandchildren. She has a bachelor's degree in Accounting and lives in Texas. As a teenager, she competed in and won a series of local, state, and national singing competitions. Today, she uses her writing and singing talents to serve God.

PLEASE RATE MY BOOK

I would be honored if you would please take a few moments to rate my book on Amazon.com.

Or, if you're in any of these countries, please use these Amazon sites:

Amazon.ca (Canada)　　　Amazon.co.uk (U.K.)
Amazon.com.au (Australia)　Amazon.fr (France)
Amazon.de (Germany)　　Amazon.co.jp (Japan)
Amazon.com.mx (Mexico)　Amazon.es (Spain)

A 5-star rating *and* a short review (e.g. "Thoroughly enjoyed it!" or "Very helpful!") would be much appreciated. I welcome longer comments as well.

I'm committed to providing the best value to my readers, and your thoughts can make that possible. Please contact me directly with any additional feedback that may be helpful in improving future editions. You can reach me at the email address below.

Please stay in touch! If you haven't already, connect with me on Instagram. It is a blessing to have you as a friend.

Thank you very much,

Kimberly A. Sanford

Author

Kimberly@WisdomWithLove.com
Instagram: Kimberly_A_Sanford

www.ingramcontent.com/pod-product-compliance
Lightning Source LLC
Chambersburg PA
CBHW050557170426
43201CB00011B/1723